# Crossing Open Ground

By the Same Author

*Desert Notes: Reflections in the Eye of a Raven*

*Giving Birth to Thunder, Sleeping with His Daughter: Coyote Builds North America*

*Of Wolves and Men*

*River Notes: The Dance of Herons*

*Winter Count*

*Arctic Dreams*

VINTAGE BOOKS

A DIVISION OF RANDOM HOUSE, INC.

NEW YORK

# CROSSING OPEN GROUND

***Barry Lopez***

FIRST VINTAGE BOOKS EDITION, MAY 1989

 Published in the United States by Random House, Inc., New York. Originally published, in hardcover, by Charles Scribner's Sons, New York, in 1988. This edition is reprinted by arrangement with Charles Scribner's Sons, an imprint of Macmillan Publishing Company.

The articles and essays in this collection first appeared in the following publications, whose editors and staffs I wish to gratefully acknowledge: "The Stone Horse" in *Antaeus* (Autumn 1986); "A Reflection on White Geese" under a different title and in a slightly different form in *Outside* (October 1982); "Gone Back into the Earth" under a different title in *Notre Dame Magazine* (May 1981); "Trying the Land" in *Harper's* (February 1979); "Landscape and Narrative" under a different title in *Harper's* (December 1984); "Yukon-Charley: The Shape of Wilderness" under a different title and in a different form in *Wilderness* (Fall 1982); "Borders" in *Country Journal* (September 1981); "The Bull Rider" in *Chouteau Review* (Spring 1978); "A Presentation of Whales" in *Harper's* (March 1980); "Children in the Woods" in Pacific Northwest (April 1982); "The Lives of Seals" in a slightly different form in *Science/82* (November 1982); "Searching for Ancestors" in *Outside* (April 1983); "Grown Men" in *Notre Dame Magazine* (October 1979); and "The Passing Wisdom of Birds" in a slightly different form in *Orion Nature Quarterly* (Autumn 1985).

"The Stone Horse" appeared in *The Best American Essays 1987*, selected by Robert Atwan and Gay Talese, published by Ticknor & Fields. I was able to research this essay while working on a related article for *National Geographic* Magazine and wish to thank the Society and the editors of the magazine for their support.

"The Bull Rider" is dedicated to Brian Claypool (1953–1979). "The Stone Horse" is dedicated to my brother, Dennis Lopez.

LIBRARY OF CONGRESS CATALOGING-IN-PUBLICATION DATA
Lopez, Barry Holstun,
1945–Crossing open ground.
Reprint. Originally published: 1978.
I. Title.
[PS3562.O67C7] 1989 814'.54 88-82390
ISBN 0-679-72183-5

Manufactured in the United States of America
10 9 8 7 6 5 4 3 2 1

*To the men and women with whom I've traveled*
*and to the editors with whom I've worked,*
*especially L. S.*

# Contents

## Author's Note

In selecting work from the recent past, I have not considered either travel pieces or essays and articles I thought would be redundant or which, on reflection, did not seem substantial. I have rewritten each piece, at least slightly. Some required emendations in phrasing; one or two needed additional work to eliminate summary paragraphs which, in the collection taken as a whole, seemed unnecessary.

# Crossing Open Ground

# The Stone Horse

THE DESERTS of southern California, the high, relatively cooler and wetter Mojave and the hotter, dryer Sonoran to the south of it, carry the signatures of many cultures. Prehistoric rock drawings in the Mojave's Coso Range, probably the greatest concentration of petroglyphs in North America, are at least three thousand years old. Big game hunting cultures that flourished six or seven thousand years before that are known from broken spear tips, choppers, and burins left scattered along the shores of great Pleistocene lakes, long since evaporated. Weapons and tools discovered at China

Lake may be thirty thousand years old; and worked stone from a quarry in the Calico Mountains is, some argue, evidence that human beings were here more than two hundred thousand years ago.

Because of the long-term stability of such arid environments, much of this prehistoric stone evidence still lies exposed on the ground, accessible to anyone who passes by—the studious, the acquisitive, the indifferent, the merely curious. Archaeologists do not agree on the sequence of cultural history beyond about twelve thousand years ago, but it is clear that these broken bits of chalcedony, chert, and obsidian, like the animal drawings and geometric designs etched on walls of basalt throughout the desert, anchor the earliest threads of human history, the first record of human endeavor here.

Western man did not enter the California desert until the end of the eighteenth century, 250 years after Coronado brought his soldiers into the Zuni pueblos in a bewildered search for the cities of Cibola. The earliest appraisals of the land were cursory, hurried. People traveled *through* it, en route to Santa Fe or the California coastal settlements. Only miners tarried. In 1823 what had been Spain's became Mexico's and in 1848 what had been Mexico's became America's; but the bare, jagged mountains and dry lake beds, the vast and uniform plains of creosote bush and yucca plants, remained as obscure as the northern Sudan until the end of the nineteenth century.

Before 1940 the tangible evidence of twentieth-century man's passage here consisted of very little—the hard tracery of travel corridors; the widely scattered, relatively insignificant evidence of mining operations; and the fair expanse of irrigated fields at the desert's periphery. In the space of a hundred years or so the wagon roads were paved, railroads were laid down, and canals and high-tension lines were built to bring water and electricity across the desert to Los Angeles from the Colorado River. The dark mouths of gold, talc, and tin mines yawned from the bony flanks of desert ranges. Dust-encrusted chemical plants stood at work on the lonely edges of dry lake beds. And crops of grapes, lettuce, dates, alfalfa, and cotton covered the Coachella and Imperial valleys, north and south of the Salton Sea, and the Palo Verde Valley along the Colorado.

These developments proceeded with little or no awareness of earlier human occupations by cultures that preceded those of the historic Indians—the Mohave, the Chemehuevi, the Quechan. (Extensive irrigation began to actually change the climate of the Sonoran Desert, and human settlements, the railroads, and farming introduced many new, successful plants and animals into the region.)

During World War II, the American military moved into the desert in great force, to train troops and to test equipment. They found the clear weather conducive to year-round flying, the dry air, and isolation very attractive. After the war, a complex of training grounds, storage facilities, and gunnery and test ranges was permanently settled on more than three million acres of military reservations. Few perceived the extent or significance of the destruction of aboriginal sites that took place during tank maneuvers and bombing runs or in the laying out of highways, railroads, mining districts, and irrigated fields. The few who intuited that something like an American Dordogne Valley lay exposed here were (only) amateur archaeologists; even they reasoned that the desert was too vast for any of this to matter.

After World War II, people began moving out of the crowded Los Angeles basin into homes in Lucerne, Apple, and Antelope valleys in the western Mojave. They emigrated as well to a stretch of resort land at the foot of the San Jacinto Mountains that included Palm Springs, and farther out to old railroad and military towns like Twentynine Palms and Barstow. People also began exploring the desert, at first in military-surplus jeeps and then with a variety of all-terrain and off-road vehicles that became available in the 1960s. By the mid-1970s, the number of people using such vehicles for desert recreation had increased exponentially. Most came and went in innocent curiosity; the few who didn't wreaked a havoc all out of proportion to their numbers. The disturbance of previously isolated archaeological sites increased by an order of magnitude. Many sites were vandalized before archaeologists, themselves late to the desert, had any firm grasp of the bounds of human history in the desert. It was as though in the same moment an Aztec library had been discovered intact various lacunae had begun to appear.

The vandalism was of three sorts: the general disturbance usually caused by souvenir hunters and by the curious and the oblivious; the wholesale stripping of a place by professional thieves for black-market sale and trade; and outright destruction, in which vehicles were actually used to ram and trench an area. By 1980, the Bureau of Land Management estimated that probably thirty-five percent of the archaeological sites in the desert had been vandalized. The destruction at some places by rifles and shotguns, or by power winches mounted on vehicles, was, if one cared for history, demoralizing to behold.

In spite of public education, land closures, and stricter law enforcement in recent years, the BLM estimates that, annually, about one percent of the archaeological record in the desert continues to be destroyed or stolen.

## 2

A BLM ARCHAEOLOGIST told me, with understandable reluctance, where to find the intaglio. I spread my Automobile Club of Southern California map of Imperial County out on his desk, and he traced the route with a pink felt-tip pen. The line crossed Interstate 8 and then turned west along the Mexican border.

"You can't drive any farther than about here," he said, marking a small *x*. "There's boulders in the wash. You walk up past them."

On a separate piece of paper he drew a route in a smaller scale that would take me up the arroyo to a certain point where I was to cross back east, to another arroyo. At its head, on higher ground just to the north, I would find the horse.

"It's tough to spot unless you know it's there. Once you pick it up . . ." He shook his head slowly, in a gesture of wonder at its existence.

I waited until I held his eye. I assured him I would not tell anyone else how to get there. He looked at me with stoical despair, like a man who had been robbed twice, whose belief in human beings was offered without conviction.

I did not go until the following day because I wanted to see it at dawn. I ate breakfast at 4 A.M. in El Centro and then drove south. The route was easy to follow, though the last section of road proved difficult, broken and drifted over with sand in some spots. I came to the barricade of boulders and parked. It was light enough by then to find my way over the ground with little trouble. The contours of the landscape were stark, without any masking vegetation. I worried only about rattlesnakes.

I traversed the stone plain as directed, but, in spite of the frankness of the land, I came on the horse unawares. In the first moment of recognition I was without feeling. I recalled later being startled, and that I held my breath. It was laid out on the ground with its head to the east, three times life size. As I took in its outline I felt a growing concentration of all my senses, as though my attentiveness to the pale rose color of the morning sky and other peripheral images had now ceased to be important. I was aware that I was straining for sound in the windless air and I felt the uneven pressure of the earth hard against my feet. The horse, outlined in a standing profile on the dark ground, was as vivid before me as a bed of tulips.

I've come upon animals suddenly before, and felt a similar tension, a precipitate heightening of the senses. And I have felt the inexplicable but sharply boosted intensity of a wild moment in the bush, where it is not until some minutes later that you discover the source of electricity—the warm remains of a grizzly bear kill, or the still moist tracks of a wolverine.

But this was slightly different. I felt I had stepped into an unoccupied corridor. I had no familiar sense of history, the temporal structure in which to think: This horse was made by Quechan people three hundred years ago. I felt instead a headlong rush of images: people hunting wild horses with spears on the Pleistocene veld of southern California; Cortés riding across the causeway into Montezuma's Tenochtitlán; a short-legged Comanche, astride his horse like some sort of ferret, slashing through cavalry lines of young men who rode like farmers. A hoof exploding past my face one morning in a corral in Wyoming. These images had the weight and silence of stone.

When I released my breath, the images softened. My initial feeling, of facing a wild animal in a remote region, was replaced with a calm sense of antiquity. It was then that I became conscious, like an ordinary tourist, of what was before me, and thought: This horse was probably laid out by Quechan people. But when, I wondered? The first horses they saw, I knew, might have been those that came north from Mexico in 1692 with Father Eusebio Kino. But Cocopa people, I recalled, also came this far north on occasion, to fight with their neighbors, the Quechan. And *they* could have seen horses with Melchior Díaz, at the mouth of the Colorado River in the fall of 1540. So, it could be four hundred years old. (No one in fact knows.)

I still had not moved. I took my eyes off the horse for a moment to look south over the desert plain into Mexico, to look east past its head at the brightening sunrise, to situate myself. Then, finally, I brought my trailing foot slowly forward and stood erect. Sunlight was running like a thin sheet of water over the stony ground and it threw the horse into relief. It looked as though no hand had ever disturbed the stones that gave it its form.

The horse had been brought to life on ground called desert pavement, a tight, flat matrix of small cobbles blasted smooth by sand-laden winds. The uniform, monochromatic blackness of the stones, a patina of iron and magnesium oxides called desert varnish, is caused by long-term exposure to the sun. To make this type of low-relief ground glyph, or intaglio, the artist either selectively turns individual stones over to their lighter side or removes areas of stone to expose the lighter soil underneath, creating a negative image. This horse, about eighteen feet from brow to rump and eight feet from withers to hoof, had been made in the latter way, and its outline was bermed at certain points with low ridges of stone a few inches high to enhance its three-dimensional qualities. (The left side of the horse was in full profile; each leg was extended at 90 degrees to the body and fully visible, as though seen in three-quarter profile.)

I was not eager to move. The moment I did I would be back in the flow of time, the horse no longer quivering in the same way before me. I did not want to feel again the sequence of quotidian events—to be drawn off into deliberation and analysis. A human being, a four-footed animal, the open land. That was all that was present—and a "thoughtless" understanding of the very old desires bearing on this particular animal: to hunt it, to render it, to fathom it, to subjugate it, to honor it, to take it as a companion.

What finally made me move was the light. The sun now filled the shallow basin of the horse's body. The weighted line of the stone berm created the illusion of a mane and the distinctive roundness of an equine belly. The change in definition impelled me. I moved to the left, circling past its rump, to see how the light might flesh the horse out from various points of view. I circled it completely before squatting on my haunches. Ten or fifteen minutes later I chose another view. The third time I moved, to a point near the rear hooves, I spotted a stone tool at my feet. I stared at it a long while, more in awe than disbelief, before reaching out to pick it up. I turned it over in my left palm and took it between my fingers to feel its cutting edge. It is always difficult, especially with something so portable, to rechannel the desire to steal.

I spent several hours with the horse. As I changed positions and as the angle of the light continued to change I noticed a number of things. The angle at which the pastern carried the hoof away from the ankle was perfect. Also, stones had been placed within the image to suggest, at precisely the right spot, the left shoulder above the foreleg. The line that joined thigh and hock was similarly accurate. The muzzle alone seemed distorted—but perhaps these stones had been moved by a later hand. It was an admirably accurate representation, but not what a breeder would call perfect conformation. There was the suggestion of a bowed neck and an undershot jaw, and the tail, as full as a winter coyote's, did not appear to be precisely to scale.

The more I thought about it, the more I felt I was looking at an individual horse, a unique combination of generic and specific detail. It was easy to imagine one of Kino's horses as a model, or a horse that ran off from one of Coronado's columns. What kind of horses would these have been, I wondered? In the sixteenth century the most sought-after horses in Europe were Spanish, the offspring of Arabian stock and Barbary horses that the Moors brought to Iberia and bred to the older, eastern European strains brought in by the Romans. The model for this horse, I speculated, could easily have been a palomino, or a descendant of horses trained for lion-hunting in North Africa.

A few generations ago, cowboys, cavalry quartermasters, and draymen would have taken this horse before me under consideration and not let up their scrutiny until they had its heritage fixed to their satisfaction. Today, the distinction between draft and harness horses is arcane knowledge, and no image may come to mind for a blue roan or a claybank horse. The loss of such refinement in everyday conversation leaves me unsettled. People praise the Eskimo's ability to distinguish among forty types of snow but forget the skill of others who routinely differentiate between overo and tobiano pintos. Such distinctions are made for the same reason. You have to do it to be able to talk clearly about the world.

For parts of two years I worked as a horse wrangler and packer in Wyoming. It is dim knowledge now; I would have to think to remember if a buckskin was a kind of dun horse. And I couldn't throw a double-diamond hitch over a set of panniers—the packer's basic tie-down—without guidance. As I squatted there in the desert, however, these more personal memories seemed tenuous in comparison with the sweep of this animal in human time. My memories had no depth. I thought of the Hittite cavalry riding against the Syrians 3500 years ago. And the first of the Chinese emperors, Ch'in Shih Huang, buried in Shensi Province in 210 B.C. with thousands of life-size horses and soldiers, a terra-cotta guardian army. What could I know of what was in the mind of whoever made this horse? Was there some racial memory of it as an animal that had once fed the artist's ancestors and then disappeared from North America? And then returned in this strange alliance with another race of men?

Certainly, whoever it was, the artist had observed the animal very closely. Certainly the animal's speed had impressed him. Among the first things the Quechan would have learned from an encounter with Kino's horses was that their own long-distance runners—men who could run down mule deer—were no match for this animal.

From where I squatted I could look far out over the Mexican plain. Juan Bautista de Anza passed this way in 1774, extending El Camino Real into Alta California from Sinaloa. He was followed by others, all of them astride the magical horse; *gente de razón,* the people of reason, coming into the country of *los primitivos.* The horse, like the stone animals of Egypt, urged these memories upon me. And as I drew them up from some forgotten corner of my mind—huge horses carved in the white chalk downs of southern England by an Iron Age people; Spanish horses rearing and wheeling in fear before alligators in Florida—the images seemed tethered before me. With this sense of proportion, a memory of my own—the morning I almost lost my face to a horse's hoof—now had somewhere to fit.

I rose up and began to walk slowly around the horse again. I had taken the first long measure of it and was looking now for a way to depart, a new angle of light, a fading of the image itself before the rising sun, that would break its hold on me. As I circled, feeling both heady and serene at the encounter, I realized again how strangely vivid it was. It had been created on a barren bajada between two arroyos, as nondescript a place as one could imagine. The only plant life here was a few wands of ocotillo cactus. The ground beneath my shoes was so hard it wouldn't take the print of a heavy animal even after a rain. The only sounds I had heard here were the voices of quail.

The archaeologist had been correct. For all its forcefulness, the horse is inconspicuous. If you don't care to see it you can walk right past it. That pleases him, I think. Unmarked on this bleak shoulder of the plain, the site signals to no one; so he wants no protective fences here, no informative plaque, to act as beacons. He would rather take a chance that no motorcyclist, no aimless wanderer with a flair for violence and a depth of ignorance, will ever find his way here.

The archaeologist had given me something before I left his office that now seemed peculiar—an aerial photograph of the horse. It is widely believed that an aerial view of an intaglio provides a fair and accurate description. It does not. In the photograph the horse looks somewhat crudely constructed; from the ground it appears far more deftly rendered. The photograph is of a single moment, and in that split second the horse seems vaguely impotent. I watched light pool in the intaglio at dawn; I imagine you could watch it withdraw at dusk and sense the same animation I did. In those prolonged moments its shape and so, too, its general character changed—noticeably. The living quality of the image, its immediacy to the eye, was brought out by the light-in-time, not, at least here, in the camera's frozen instant.

Intaglios, I thought, were never meant to be seen by gods in the sky above. They were meant to be seen by people on the ground, over a long period of shifting light. This could even be true of the huge figures on the Plain of Nazca in Peru, where people could walk for the length of a day beside them. It is our own impatience that leads us to think otherwise.

This process of abstraction, almost unintentional, drew me gradually away from the horse. I came to a position of attention at the edge of the sphere of its influence. With a slight bow I paid my respects to the horse, its maker, and the history of us all, and departed.

## 3

A SHORT DISTANCE away I stopped the car in the middle of the road to make a few notes. I had not been able to write down what I was thinking when I was with the horse. It would have seemed disrespectful, and it would have required another kind of attention. So now I patiently drained my memory of the details it had fastened itself upon. The road I'd stopped on was adjacent to the All American Canal, the major source of water for the Imperial and Coachella valleys. The water flowed west placidly. A disjointed flock of coots, small, dark birds with white bills, was paddling against the current, foraging in the rushes.

I was peripherally aware of the birds as I wrote, the only movement in the desert; and of a series of sounds from a village a half-mile away. The first sounds from this collection of ramshackle houses in a grove of cottonwoods were the distracted dawn voices of dogs. I heard them intermingled with the cries of a rooster. Later, the high-pitched voices of children calling out to each other came disembodied through the dry desert air. Now, a little after seven, I could hear someone practicing on the trumpet, the same rough phrases played over and over. I suddenly remembered how as children we had tried to get the rhythm of a galloping horse with hands against our thighs, or by fluttering our tongues against the roofs of our mouths.

After the trumpet, the impatient calls of adults, summoning children. Sunday morning. Wood smoke hung like a lens in the trees. The first car starts—a cold, eight-cylinder engine, of Chrysler extraction perhaps, goosed to life, then throttled back to murmur through dual mufflers, the obbligato music of a shade-tree mechanic. The rote bark of mongrel dogs at dawn, the jagged outcries of men and women, an engine coming to life. Like a thousand villages from West Virginia to Guadalajara.

I finished my notes—where was I going to find a description of the horses that came north with the conquistadors? Did their manes come forward prominently over the brow, like this one's, like the forelocks of Blackfeet and Assiniboine men in nineteeth-century paintings? I set the notes on the seat beside me.

The road followed the canal for a while and then arced north, toward Interstate 8. It was slow driving and I fell to thinking how the desert had changed since Anza had come through. New plants and animals—the MacDougall cottonwood, the English house sparrow, the chukar from India—have about them now the air of the native-born. Of the native species, some—no one knows how many—are extinct. The populations of many others, especially the animals, have been sharply reduced. The idea of a desert impoverished by agricultural poisons and varmint hunters, by off-road vehicles and military operations, did not seem as disturbing to me, however, as this other horror, now that I had been those hours with the horse. The vandals, the few who crowbar rock art off the desert's walls, who dig up graves, who punish the ground that holds intaglios, are people who devour history. Their self-centered scorn, their disrespect for ideas and images beyond their ken, create the awful atmosphere of loose ends in which totalitarianism thrives, in which the past is merely curious or wrong.

I thought about the horse sitting out there on the unprotected plain. I enumerated its qualities in my mind until a sense of its vulnerability receded and it became an anchor for something else. I remembered that history, a history like this one, which ran deeper than Mexico, deeper than the Spanish, was a kind of medicine. It permitted the great breadth of human expression to reverberate, and it did not urge you to locate its apotheosis in the present.

Each of us, individuals and civilizations, has been held upside down like Achilles in the River Styx. The artist mixing his colors in the dim light of Altamira; an Egyptian ruler lying still now, wrapped in his byssus, stored against time in a pyramid; the faded Dorset culture of the Arctic; the Hmong and Samburu and Walbiri of historic time; the modern nations. This great, imperfect stretch of human expression is the clarification and encouragement, the urging and the reminder, we call history. And it is inscribed everywhere in the face of the land, from the mountain passes of the Himalayas to a nameless bajada in the California desert.

Small birds rose up in the road ahead, startled, and flew off. I prayed no infidel would ever find that horse.

# A Reflection on White Geese

I SLOW THE CAR, downshifting from fourth to third, with the melancholic notes of Bach's sixth cello suite in my ears—a recording of Casals from 1936—and turn east, away from a volcanic ridge of black basalt. On this cool California evening, the land in the marshy valley beyond is submerged in gray light, while the far hills are yet touched by a sunset glow. To the south, out the window, Venus glistens, a white diamond at the horizon's dark lapis edge. A few feet to my left is lake water—skittish mallards and coots bolt from the cover of bulrushes and pound the air furiously to put distance between us. I am chagrined, and slow down. I have been driving like this for hours—slowed by snow in the mountains behind me, listening to the cello suites—driving hard to get here before sunset.

I shut the tape off. In the waning light I can clearly see marsh hawks swooping over oat and barley fields to the south. Last hunts of the day. The eastern sky is beginning to blush, a rose afterglow. I roll the window down. The car fills with the sounds of birds—the nasalized complaints of several hundred mallards, pintails and canvasbacks, the slap-water whirr of their half-hearted takeoffs. But underneath this sound something else is expanding, distant French horns and kettledrums.

Up ahead, on the narrow dirt causeway, I spot Frans's car. He is here for the same reason I am.* I pull up quietly and he emerges from his front seat, which he has made into a kind of photographic blind. We hug and exchange quiet words of greeting, and then turn to look at the white birds. Behind us the dark waters of Tule Lake, rippled by a faint wind, stretch off north, broken only by occasional islands of hardstem bulrush. Before us, working methodically through a field of two-row barley, the uninterrupted inquiry of their high-pitched voices lifting the night, are twenty-five thousand snow geese come down from the Siberian and Canadian Arctic. Grazing, but alert and wary in this last light.

---

*Frans Lanting's photographs, which accompanied this article, appeared in French *GEO* (December 1982) and in *Outside* (October 1982).

Frans motions wordlessly to his left; I scan that far eastern edge of Tule Lake with field glasses. One hundred thousand lesser snow geese and Ross's geese float quietly on riffles, a white crease between the dark water and the darkening hills.

THE STAGING of white geese at Tule Lake in northern California in November is one of the most imposing—and dependable—wildlife spectacles in the world. At first one thinks of it only as a phenomenon of numbers—it's been possible in recent years to see as many as three hundred thousand geese here at one time. What a visitor finds as startling, however, is the great synchronicity of their movements: long skeins of white unfurl brilliantly against blue skies and dark cumulonimbus thunderheads, birds riding the towering wash of winds. They rise from the water or fall from the sky with balletic grace, with a booming noise like rattled sheets of corrugated tin, with a furious and unmitigated energy. It is the *life* of them that takes such hold of you.

I have spent enough time with large predators to know the human predilection to overlook authority and mystery in the lives of small, gregarious animals like the goose, but its qualities are finally as subtle, its way of making a living as admirable and attractive, as the grizzly bear's.

Geese are traditional, one could even say conservative, animals. They tend to stick to the same nesting grounds and wintering areas, to the same migration routes, year after year. Males and females have identical plumage. They usually mate for life, and both sexes care for the young. In all these ways, as well as in being more at ease on land, geese differ from ducks. They differ from swans in having proportionately longer legs and shorter necks. In size they fall somewhere between the two. A mature male lesser snow goose *(Chen caerulescens)*, for example, might weigh six pounds, measure thirty inches from bill to tail and have a wingspan of three feet. A mature female would be slightly smaller and lighter by perhaps half a pound.

Taxonomists divide the geese of the Northern Hemisphere into two groups, "gray" and "black," according to the color of their bills, feet and legs. Among black geese like Canada geese and brandt they're dark. Snow geese, with rose-pink feet and legs and pink bills, are grouped with the gray geese, among whom these appendages are often brightly colored. Snow geese also commonly have rust-speckled faces, from feeding in iron-rich soils.

Before it was changed in 1971, the snow goose's scientific name, *Chen hyperborea*, reflected its high-arctic breeding heritage. The greater snow goose *(C. c. atlantica)*—a larger but far less numerous race of snow goose—breeds in northwestern Greenland and on adjacent Ellesmere, Devon and Axel Heiburg islands. The lesser snow goose breeds slightly farther south, on Baffin and Southampton islands, the east coast of Hudson Bay, and on Banks Island to the west and Wrangel Island in

Siberia. (Many people are attracted to the snow goose precisely because of its association with these little-known regions.)

There are two color phases, finally, of the lesser snow goose, blue and white. The combined population of about 1.5 million, the largest of any goose in the world, is divided into an eastern, mostly blue-phase population that winters in Texas and Louisiana, and a western, white-phase population that winters in California. (It is the latter birds that pass through Tule Lake.)

The great numbers of these highly gregarious birds can be misleading. First, we were not certain until quite recently where snow geese were nesting, or how large their breeding colonies were. The scope of the problem is suggested by the experience of a Canadian biologist, Angus Gavin. In 1941 he stumbled on what he thought was a small breeding colony of lesser snow geese, on the delta of the McConnell River on the east coast of Hudson Bay—14,000 birds. In 1961 there were still only about 35,000 birds there. But a 1968 survey showed 100,000 birds and in 1973 there were 520,000. Second, populations of arctic-breeding species like the snow goose are subject to extreme annual fluctuations, a boom-and-bust cycle tied to the unpredictable weather patterns typical of arctic ecosystems. After a series of prolonged winters, for example, when persistent spring snow cover kept birds from nesting, the Wrangel Island population of snow geese fell from 400,000 birds in 1965 to fewer than 50,000 in 1975. (By the summer of 1981 it was back up to 170,000.)

The numbers in which we see them on their wintering grounds are large enough to be comforting—it is hard at first to imagine what would threaten such flocks. Snow geese, however, face a variety of problems. The most serious is a striking loss of winter habitat. In 1900 western snow geese had more than 6200 square miles of winter habitat available to them on California's Sacramento and San Joaquin rivers. Today, ninety percent of this has been absorbed by agricultural, industrial and urban expansion. This means ninety percent of the land in central California that snow geese once depended on for food and shelter is gone. Hunters in California kill about twenty percent of the population each year and leave another four to five percent crippled to die of starvation and injuries. (An additional two to three percent dies each year of lead poisoning, from ingesting spent shot.) An unknown number are also killed by high-tension wires. In the future, geese will likely face a significant threat on their arctic breeding grounds from oil and gas exploration.

The birds also suffer from the same kinds of diseases, traumatic accidents and natural disasters that threaten all organisms. Females, for example, fiercely devoted to the potential in their egg clutches, may choose to die of exposure on their nests rather than to abandon them in an unseasonable storm.

In the light of all this, it is ironic that the one

place on earth a person might see these geese in numbers large enough to cover half the sky is, itself, a potential threat to their existence.

THE LAND now called Tule Lake National Wildlife Refuge lies in a volcanic basin, part of which was once an extensive, 2700-square-mile marshland. In 1905 the federal government began draining the area to create irrigated croplands. Marshland habitat and bird populations shrank. By 1981 only fifty-six square miles of wetland, 2 percent of the original area, was left for waterfowl. In spite of this reduction, the area, incredibly, remains an ideal spot for migratory waterfowl. On nearly any given day in the fall a visitor to the Klamath Basin might see more than a million birds—mallards, gadwalls, pintails, lesser scaups, goldeneyes, cinnamon teals, northern shovelers, redheads, canvasbacks, ruddy ducks; plus western and cackling Canada geese, white-fronted geese, Ross's geese, lesser snow geese and whistling swans. (More than 250 species of birds have been seen on or near the refuge and more than 170 nest here.)

The safety of these populations is in the hands of a resident federal manager and his staff, who must effectively balance the birds' livelihood with the demands of local farmers, who use Tule Lake's water to irrigate adjacent fields of malt barley and winter potatoes, and waterfowl hunters, some of whom come from hundreds of miles away. And there is another problem. Although the Klamath Basin is the greatest concentration point for migratory waterfowl in North America, caring well for birds here is no guarantee they will fare well elsewhere along the flyway. And a geographic concentration like this merely increases the chance of catastrophe if epidemic disease should strike.

THE FIRST TIME I visited Tule Lake I arrived early on a fall afternoon. When I asked where the snow geese were congregated I was directed to an area called the English Channel, several miles out on the refuge road. I sat there for three hours, studying the birds' landings and takeoffs, how they behaved toward each other on the water, how they shot the skies overhead. I tried to unravel and to parse the dazzling synchronicity of their movements. I am always struck anew in these moments, in observing such detail, by the way in which an animal slowly reveals itself.

Before the sun went down, I drove off to see more of the snow goose's landscape, what other animals there might be on the refuge, how the land changed at a distance from the water. I found the serpentine great blue heron, vivacious and melodious flocks of red-winged blackbirds, and that small, fierce hunter, the kestrel. Muskrats bolted across the road. At the southern end of the refuge, where cattails and bulrushes give way to rabbit brush and sage on a volcanic plain, I came upon mule deer, three does and four fawns standing still and tense in a meandering fog.

I found a room that evening in the small town of Tulelake. There'd not been, that I could recall, a moment of silence all day from these most loquacious of geese. I wondered if they were mum in the middle of the night, how quiet they were at dawn. I set the alarm for 3 A.M.

The streets of Tulelake are desolate at that hour. In that odd stillness—the stillness of moonlit horses standing asleep in fields—I drove out into the countryside, toward the refuge. It was a ride long enough to hear the first two movements of Beethoven's Fifth Symphony. I drove in a light rain, past white farmhouses framed by ornamental birches and weeping willows. In the 1860s this land was taken by force from the Modoc Indians; in the 1940s the government built a Japanese internment camp here. At this hour, however, nearly every landscape has a pervasive innocence. I passed the refuge headquarters—low shiplapped buildings, white against a dark ridge of basalt, facing a road lined with Russian olives. I drove past stout, slowly dying willows of undetermined age, trees that mark the old shoreline of Tule Lake, where it was before the reclamation project began.

The music is low, barely audible, but the enthusiasm in some of the strong passages reminds me of geese. I turn the tape off and drive a narrow, cratered road out into the refuge, feeling the car slipping sideways in the mud. Past rafts of sleeping ducks. The first geese I see surge past just overhead like white butterflies, brushing the penumbral dimness above the car's headlights. I open the window and feel the sudden assault of their voices, the dunning power of their wings hammering the air, a rush of cold wind and rain through the window. In a moment I am outside, standing in the roar. I find a comfortable, protected place in the bulrushes and wait in my parka until dawn, listening.

Their collective voice, like the cries of athletic young men at a distance, is unabated. In the darkness it is nearly all there is of them, but for an occasional and eerie passage overhead. I try to listen closely: a barking of high-voiced dogs, like terriers, the squealing of shoats. By an accident of harmonics the din rises and falls like the cheering of a crowd in a vast stadium. Whoops and shouts; startled voices of outrage, of shock.

These are not the only voices. Cackling geese pass over in the dark, their cries more tentative. Coyotes yip. Nearby some creature screeches, perhaps a mouse in the talons of a great horned owl, whose skipping hoots I have heard earlier.

A gibbous moon shines occasionally through a wind-driven overcast. Toward dawn the geese's voices fall off suddenly for a few moments. The silence seems primordial. The black sky in the east now shows blood red through scalloped shelves of cloud. It broadens into an orange flare that fades to rose and finally to the grays of dawn. The voices begin again.

I drive back into Tulelake and eat breakfast amid a throng of hunters crowding the tables of a small cafe, steaming the windows with their raucous conversation.

* * *

BOB FIELDS, the refuge manager, has agreed to take me on a tour in the afternoon. I decide to spend the morning at the refuge headquarters, reading scientific reports and speaking with biologist Ed O'Neill about the early history of Tule Lake.

O'Neill talks first about the sine qua non, a suitable expanse of water. In the American West the ownership of surface water confers the kind of political and economic power that comes elsewhere with oil wells and banks. Water is a commodity; it is expensive to maintain and its owners seek to invest the limited supply profitably. A hunting club that keeps private marshland for geese and ducks, for example, will do so only as long as they feel their hunting success warrants it. If the season is shortened or the bag limit reduced by the state—the most common ways to conserve dwindling waterfowl populations—they might find hunting no longer satisfying and sell the marsh to farmers, who will turn it into cropland. Real-estate speculators and other landowners with substantial surface-water rights rarely give the birds that depend on their lands a second thought when they're preparing to sell. As O'Neill puts it, "You can't outweigh a stack of silver dollars with a duck."

The plight of western waterfowl is made clearer by an anomaly. In the eastern United States, a natural abundance of water and the closure of many tracts of private land to hunting provide birds with a strong measure of protection. In the West, bird populations are much larger, but water is scarcer and refuge lands, because they are largely public, remain open to hunting.

By carefully adjusting the length of the hunting season and the bag limits each year, and by planting food for the birds, refuge managers try to maintain large bird populations, in part to keep private hunting clubs along the flyway enthusiastic about continuing to provide additional habitat for the birds. Without the help of private individuals, including conservation groups that own wetlands, the federal and state refuge systems simply cannot provide for the birds. (This is especially true now. The Reagan administration has proved more hostile to the preservation of federal refuges and their denizens than any American administration since the turn of the century.)

Some birds, the snow goose among them, have adapted to shortages of food and land. Deprived of the rootstocks of bulrushes and marsh grasses, snow geese in the West have switched to gleaning agricultural wastes and cropping winter wheat, a practice that has spread to the Midwest, where snow geese now feed increasingly on rice and corn. A second adjustment snow geese have made is to linger on their fall migrations and to winter over farther north. That way fewer birds end up for a shorter period of time on traditional wintering grounds, where food is scarcer each year.

As we spoke, O'Neill kept glancing out the window. He told me about having seen as many as three hundred thousand white geese there in years past. With the loss of habitat and birds spreading out now to winter along the flyway, such aggregations, he says, may never be seen again. He points out, too, looking dismayed and vaguely bitter, that these huge flocks have not been conserved for the viewer who does not hunt, for the tourist who comes to Tule Lake to see something he has only dreamed of.

We preserve them, principally, to hunt them.

IN BROAD DAYLIGHT I was able to confirm something I'd read about the constant, loud din of their voices: relatively few birds are actually vocalizing at any one time, perhaps only one in thirty. Biologists speculate that snow geese recognize each other's voices and that family units of three or four maintain contact in these vast aggregations by calling out to one another. What sounds like mindless chaos to the human ear, then, may actually be a complex pattern of solicitous cries, discretely distinguished by snow geese.

Another sound that is easier to decipher in daylight is the rising squall that signals they are leaving the water. It's like the sustained hammering of a waterfall or a wind booming in the full crowns of large trees.

One wonders, watching the geese fly off in flocks of a hundred or a thousand, if they would be quite so arresting without their stunning whiteness. When they fly with the sun behind them, the opaque white of their bodies, the white of water-polished seashells, is set off against grayer whites in their tail feathers and in their translucent, black-tipped wings. Up close these are the dense, impeccable whites of an arctic fox. Against the grays and blues of a storm-laden sky, the whiteness has a surreal glow, a brilliance without shadow.

I remember watching a large flock rise one morning from a plowed field about a mile distant. I had been watching clouds, the soft, buoyant, wind-blown edges of immaculate cumulus. The birds rose against much darker clouds to the east. There was something vaguely ominous in this apparition, as if the earth had opened and poured them forth, like a wind, a blizzard, which unfurled across the horizon above the dark soil, becoming wider and higher in the sky than my field of vision could encompass, great swirling currents of birds in a rattling of wings, one fluid recurved sweep of 10,000 passing through the open spaces in another, counterflying flock, while beyond them lattice after lattice passed like sliding walls, until in the whole sky you lost your depth of field and felt as though you were looking up from the floor of the ocean through shoals of fish.

AT REST on the water the geese drank and slept and bathed and preened. They reminded me in their ablutions of the field notes of a Hudson's Bay trader, George Barnston. He wrote of watching flocks of snow geese gathering on James Bay in 1862, in preparation for their annual two-thousand-mile, nonstop thirty-two-hour flight to the Louisiana coast. They finally left off feeding, he wrote, to smooth and dress their feathers with oil, like athletes, biding their time for a north wind. When it came they were gone, hundreds of thousands of them, leaving a coast once "widely resonant with their petulant and incessant calls" suddenly as "silent as the grave—a deserted, barren, and frozen shore."

Barnston was struck by the way snow geese did things together. No other waterfowl are as gregarious; certainly no other large bird flies as skillfully in such tight aggregations. This quality—the individual act beautifully integrated within the larger movement of the flock—is provocative. One afternoon I studied individual birds for hours as they landed and took off. I never once saw a bird on the water move over to accommodate a bird that was landing; nor a bird ever disturbed by another taking off, no matter how tightly they were bunched. In no flight overhead did I see two birds so much as brush wing tips. Certainly they must; but for the most part they are flawlessly adroit. A flock settles gently on the water like wiffling leaves; birds explode vertically with compact and furious wingbeats and then stretch out full length, airborne, rank on rank, as if the whole flock had been cleanly wedged from the surface of the water. Several thousand bank smoothly against a head wind, as precisely as though they were feathers in the wing of a single bird.

It was while I sat immersed in these details that Bob Fields walked up. After a long skyward stare he said, "I've been here for seven years. I never get tired of watching them."

We left in his small truck to drive the narrow

causeways of Tule Lake and the five adjacent federal refuges. Fields joined the U.S. Fish and Wildlife Service in 1958, at the age of twenty-two. His background is in range biology and plant ecology as well as waterfowl management. Before he came to Tule Lake in 1974, to manage the Klamath Basin refuges, he worked on the National Bison Range in Montana and on the Charles Sheldon Antelope Range in Nevada.

In 1975 a group of visitors who would profoundly affect Fields arrived at Tule Lake. They were Eskimos, from the Yukon-Kuskokwim delta of Alaska. They had come to see how the geese populations, which they depend on for food, were being managed. In the few days they were together, Fields came to understand that the Eskimos were appalled by the waste they saw at Tule Lake, by the number of birds hunters left crippled and unretrieved, and were surprised that hunters took only the breast meat and threw the rest of the bird away. On the other hand, the aggregations of geese they saw were so extensive they believed someone was fooling them—surely, they thought, so many birds could never be found in one place.

The experience with the Eskimos—Fields traveled north to see the Yukon-Kuskokwim country and the Eskimos returned to Tule Lake in 1977—focused his career as had no other event. In discussions with the Eskimos he found himself talking with a kind of hunter he rarely encountered anymore—humble men with a respect for the birds and a sense of responsibility toward them. That the Eskimos were dumbstruck at the number of birds led him to a more sobering thought: if he failed here as a refuge manager, his failure would run the length of the continent.

In the years following, Fields gained a reputation as a man who cared passionately for the health and welfare of waterfowl populations. He tailored, with the help of assistant refuge manager Homer McCollum, a model hunting program at Tule Lake, but he is candid in expressing his distaste for a type of hunter he still meets too frequently—belligerent, careless people for whom hunting is simply violent recreation; people who trench and rut the refuge's roads in oversize four-wheel-drive vehicles, who are ignorant of hunting laws or who delight in breaking them as part of a "game" they play with refuge personnel.

At one point in our afternoon drive, Fields and I were watching a flock of geese feeding in a field of oats and barley on the eastern edge of the refuge. We watched in silence for a long time. I said something about the way birds can calm you, how the graceful way they define the sky can draw irritation right out of you. He looked over at me and smiled and nodded. A while later, still watching the birds, he said, "I have known all along there was more to it than managing the birds so they could be killed by some macho hunter." It was the Eskimos who gave him a sense of how a hunter should behave, and their awe that rekindled his own desire to see the birds preserved.

As we drove back across the refuge, Fields spoke about the changes that had occurred in the Klamath

Basin since the federal reclamation project began in 1905. Most of the native grasses—blue bench wheat grass, Great Basin wild rye—are gone. A visitor notices foreign plants in their place, like cheatgrass. And introduced species like the ring-necked pheasant and the muskrat, which bores holes in the refuge dikes and disrupts the pattern of drainage. And the intrusion of high-tension power lines, which endanger the birds and which Fields has no budget to bury. And the presence of huge pumps that circulate water from Tule Lake to farmers in the valley, back and forth, back and forth, before pumping it west to Lower Klamath Refuge.

It is over these evolving, occasionally uneasy relationships between recent immigrants and the original inhabitants that Fields keeps watch. I say goodbye to him at his office, to the world of bird poachers, lead poisoning, and politically powerful hunting and agricultural lobbies he deals with every day. When I shake his hand I find myself wanting to thank him for the depth with which he cares for the birds, and for the intelligence that allows him to disparage not hunting itself but the lethal acts of irresponsible and thoughtless people.

I STILL HAVE a few hours before I meet Frans for dinner. I decide to drive out to the east of the refuge, to a low escarpment which bears the carvings of Indians who lived in this valley before white men arrived. I pass by open fields where horses and beef cattle graze and cowbirds flock after seeds. Red-tailed hawks are perched on telephone poles, watching for field rodents. A light rain has turned to snow.

The brooding face of the escarpment has a prehistoric quality. It is secured behind a chain link fence topped with barbed wire, but the evidence of vandals who have broken past it to knock off souvenir petroglyphs is everywhere. The castings of barn owls, nesting in stone pockets above, are spread over the ground. I open some of them to see what the owls have been eating. Meadow voles. Deer mice.

The valley before me has darkened. I know somewhere out there, too far away to see now, long scarves of snow geese are riding and banking against these rising winds, and that they are aware of the snow. In a few weeks Tule Lake will be frozen and they will be gone. I turn back to the wall of petroglyphs. The carvings relate, apparently, to the movement of animals through this land hundreds of years ago. The people who made them made their clothing and shelters, even their cooking containers, from the lake's tule reeds. When the first white man arrived—Peter Ogden, in 1826—he found them wearing blankets of duck and goose feathers. In the years since, the complex interrelationships of the Modoc with this land, largely unrecorded to begin with, have disappeared. The land itself has been turned to agriculture, with a portion set aside for certain species of birds that have passed through this valley for no one knows how many centuries. The hunters have become farmers, the farmers landowners. Their sons have gone to the cities and become businessmen, and the sons of these men have returned with guns, to take advantage of an old urge, to hunt. But more than a few come back with a poor knowledge of the birds, the land, the reason for killing. It is by now a familiar story, for which birds pay with their lives.

The old argument, that geese must be killed for their own good, to manage the size of their populations, founders on two points. Snow goose populations rise and fall precipitously because of their arctic breeding pattern. No group of hunters can "fine-tune" such a basic element of their ecology. Second, the artificial control of their numbers only augments efforts to continue draining wetlands.

We must search in our way of life, I think, for substantially more here than economic expansion and continued good hunting. We need to look for a set of relationships similar to the ones Fields admired among the Eskimos. We grasp what is beautiful in a flight of snow geese rising against an overcast sky as easily as we grasp the beauty in a cello suite; and intuit, I believe, that if we allow these things to be destroyed or degraded for economic or frivolous reasons we will become deeply and strangely impoverished.

I HAD SEEN little of my friend Frans in three days. At dinner he said he wanted to tell me of the Oostvaardersplassen in Holland. It has become a major stopover for waterfowl in northern Europe, a marsh that didn't even exist ten years ago. Birds hardly anyone has seen in Holland since the time of Napoleon are there now. Peregrine falcons, snowy egrets and European sea eagles have returned.

I drive away from the escarpment holding tenaciously to this image of reparation.

# Gone Back into the Earth

I AM UP TO MY WAIST in a basin of cool, acid-clear water, at the head of a box canyon some 600 feet above the Colorado River. I place my outstretched hands flat against a terminal wall of dark limestone which rises more than a hundred feet above me, and down which a sheet of water falls—the thin creek in whose pooled waters I now stand. The water splits at my fingertips into wild threads; higher up, a warm canyon wind lifts water off the limestone in a fine spray; these droplets intercept and shatter sunlight. Down, down another four waterfalls and fern-shrouded pools below, the water spills into an eddy of the Colorado River, in the shadow of a huge boulder. Our boat is tied there.

This lush crease in the surface of the earth is a cleft in the precipitous desert walls of Arizona's Grand Canyon. Its smooth outcrops of purple-tinged travertine stone, its heavy air rolled in the languid perfume of columbine, struck by the sharp notes of a water ouzel, the trill of a disturbed black phoebe—all this has a name: Elves Chasm.

A few feet to my right, a preacher from Maryland is staring straight up at a blue sky, straining to see what flowers those are that nod at the top of the falls. To my left a freelance automobile mechanic from Colorado sits with an impish smile by helleborine orchids. Behind, another man, a builder and sometime record producer from New York, who comes as often as he can to camp and hike in the Southwest, stands immobile at the pool's edge.

Sprawled shirtless on a rock is our boatman. He has led twelve or fifteen of us on the climb up from the river. The Colorado entrances him. He has a well-honed sense of the ridiculous, brought on, one believes, by so much time in the extreme remove of this canyon.

In our descent we meet others in our group who stopped climbing at one of the lower pools. At the second to the last waterfall, a young woman with short hair and dazzling blue eyes walks with me back into the canyon's narrowing V. We wade into a still pool, swim a few strokes to its head, climb over a boulder, swim across a second pool and then stand together, giddy, in the press of limestone, beneath the deafening cascade—filled with euphoria.

One at a time we bolt and glide, fishlike, back across the pool, grounding in fine white gravel. We wade the second pool and continue our descent, stopping to marvel at the strategy of a barrel cactus and at the pale shading of color in the ledges to which we cling. We share few words. We know hardly anything of each other. We share the country.

The group of us who have made this morning climb are in the middle of a ten-day trip down the Colorado River. Each day we are upended, if not by some element of the landscape itself then by what the landscape does, visibly, to each of us. It has snapped us like fresh-laundered sheets.

AFTER LUNCH, we reboard three large rubber rafts and enter the Colorado's quick, high flow. The river has not been this high or fast since Glen Canyon Dam—135 miles above Elves Chasm, 17 miles above our starting point at Lee's Ferry—was closed in 1963. Jumping out ahead of us, with its single oarsman and three passengers, is our fourth craft, a twelve-foot rubber boat, like a water strider with a steel frame. In Sockdolager Rapid the day before, one of its welds burst and the steel pieces were bent apart. (Sockdolager: a nineteenth-century colloquialism for knockout punch.)

Such groups as ours, the members all but unknown to each other on the first day, almost always grow close, solicitous of each other, during their time together. They develop a humor that informs similar journeys everywhere, a humor founded in tomfoolery, in punning, in a continuous parody of the life-in-civilization all have so recently (and gleefully) left. Such humor depends on context, on an accretion of small, shared events; it seems silly to those who are not there. It is not, of course. Any more than that moment of fumbling awe one feels on seeing the Brahma schist at the dead bottom of the canyon's Inner Gorge. Your fingertips graze the 1.9-billion-year-old stone as the boat drifts slowly past.

With the loss of self-consciousness, the landscape opens.

There are forty-one of us, counting a crew of six. An actor from Florida, now living in Los Angeles. A medical student and his wife. A supervisor from Virginia's Department of Motor Vehicles. A health-store owner from Chicago. An editor from New York and his young son.

That kind of diversity seems normal in groups that seek such vacations—to trek in the Himalaya, to dive in the Sea of Cortez, to go birding in the Arctic. We are together for two reasons: to run the Colorado River, and to participate with jazz musician Paul Winter, who initiated the trip, in a music workshop.

Winter is an innovator and a listener. He had thought for years about coming to the Grand Canyon, about creating music here in response to this particular landscape—collared lizards and prickly pear cactus, Anasazi

Indian ruins and stifling heat. But most especially he wanted music evoked by the river and the walls that flew up from its banks—Coconino sandstone on top of Hermit shale on top of the Supai formations, stone exposed to sunlight, a bloom of photons that lifted colors—saffron and ochre, apricot, madder orange, pearl and gray green, copper reds, umber and terra-cotta browns—and left them floating in the air.

Winter was searching for a reintegration of music, landscape and people. For resonance. Three or four times during the trip he would find it for sustained periods: drifting on a quiet stretch of water below Bass Rapids with oboist Nancy Rumbel and cellist David Darling; in a natural amphitheater high in the Muav limestone of Matkatameba Canyon; on the night of a full June moon with euphonium player Larry Roark in Blacktail Canyon.

Winter's energy and passion, and the strains of solo and ensemble music, were sewn into the trip like prevailing winds, like the canyon wren's clear, whistled, descending notes, his glissando—seemingly present, close by or at a distance, whenever someone stopped to listen.

But we came and went, too, like the swallows and swifts that flicked over the water ahead of the boats, intent on private thoughts.

ON THE SECOND DAY of the trip we stopped at Redwall Cavern, an undercut recess that spans a beach of fine sand, perhaps 500 feet wide by 150 feet deep. Winter intends to record here, but the sand absorbs too much sound. Unfazed, the others toss a Frisbee, practice Tai-chi, jog, meditate, play recorders, and read novels.

No other animal but the human would bring to bear so many activities, from so many different cultures and levels of society, with so much energy, so suddenly in a new place. And no other animal, the individuals so entirely unknown to each other, would chance together something so unknown as this river journey. In this frenetic activity and difference seems a suggestion of human evolution and genuine adventure. We are not the first down this river, but in the slooshing of human hands at the water's edge, the swanlike notes of an oboe, the occasional hugs among those most afraid of the rapids, there *is* exploration.

Each day we see or hear something that astounds us. The thousand-year-old remains of an Anasazi footbridge, hanging in twilight shadow high in the canyon wall above Harding Rapid. Deer Creek Falls, where we stand knee-deep in turquoise water encircled by a rainbow. Havasu Canyon, wild with grapevines, cottonwoods and velvet ash, speckled dace and mule deer, wild grasses and crimson monkey flowers. Each evening we enjoy a vespers: cicadas and crickets, mourning doves, vermilion flycatchers. And the wind, for which chimes are hung in a salt cedar. These notes leap above the splash and rattle, the grinding of water and the roar of rapids.

The narrow, damp, hidden worlds of the side canyons, with their scattered shards of Indian pottery and ghost imprints of 400-million-year-old nautiloids, open onto the larger world of the Colorado River itself; but nothing conveys to us how far into the earth's surface we have come. Occasionally we glimpse the South Rim, four or five thousand feet above. From the rims the canyon seems oceanic; at the surface of the river the feeling is intimate. To someone up there with binoculars we seem utterly remote down here. It is this known dimension of distance and time and the perplexing question posed by the canyon itself—What is consequential? (in one's life, in the life of human beings, in the life of a planet)—that reverberate constantly, and make the human inclination to judge (another person, another kind of thought) seem so eerie.

Two kinds of time pass here: sitting at the edge of a sun-warmed pool watching blue dragonflies and black tadpoles. And the rapids: down the glassy-smooth tongue into a yawing trench, climb a ten-foot wall of standing water and fall into boiling, ferocious hydraulics, sucking whirlpools, drowned voices, stopped hearts. Rapids can fold and shatter boats and take lives if the boatman enters at the wrong point or at the wrong angle.

Some rapids, like one called Hermit, seem more dangerous than they are and give us great roller-coaster rides. Others—Hance, Crystal, Upset—seem less spectacular, but are technically difficult. At Crystal, our boat screeches and twists against its frame. Its nose crumples like cardboard in the trough; our boatman makes the critical move to the right with split-second timing and we are over a standing wave and into the haystacks of white water, safely into the tail waves. The boatman's eyes cease to blaze.

The first few rapids—Badger Creek and Soap Creek—do not overwhelm us. When we hit the Inner Gorge—Granite Falls, Unkar Rapid, Horn Creek Rapid—some grip the boat, rigid and silent. (On the ninth day, when we are about to run perhaps the most formidable rapid, Lava Falls, the one among us who has had the greatest fear is calm, almost serene. In the last days, it is hard to overestimate what the river and the music and the unvoiced concern for each other have washed out.)

THERE ARE THREATS to this separate world of the Inner Gorge. Down inside it one struggles to maintain a sense of what they are, how they impinge.

In 1963, Glen Canyon Dam cut off the canyon's natural flow of water. Spring runoffs of more than two hundred thousand cubic feet per second ceased to roar through the gorge, clearing the main channel of rock and stones washed down from the side canyons. Fed now from the bottom of Lake Powell backed up behind the dam, the river is no longer a warm, silt-laden habitat for Colorado squawfish, razorback sucker and several kinds of chub, but a cold, clear habitat for trout. With no annual scouring and a subsequent deposition of fresh sand, the beaches show the evidence of continuous human use: they are eroding. The postflood eddies where squawfish bred have disappeared. Tamarisk (salt cedar) and camel thorn, both exotic plants formerly washed out with the spring floods, have gained an apparently permanent foothold. At the old high-water mark, catclaw acacia, mesquite and Apache plume are no longer watered and are dying out.

On the rim, far removed above, such evidence of human tampering seems, and perhaps is, pernicious. From the river, another change is more wrenching. It floods the system with a kind of panic that in other animals induces nausea and the sudden evacuation of the bowels: it is the descent of helicopters. Their sudden arrival in the canyon evokes not jeers but staring. The violence is brutal, an intrusion as criminal and as random as rape. When the helicopter departs, its rotorwind walloping against the stone walls, I want to wash the sound off my skin.

The canyon finally absorbs the intrusion. I focus quietly each day on the stone, the breathing of time locked up here, back to the Proterozoic, before there were seashells. Look up to wisps of high cirrus overhead, the hint of a mare's tail sky. Close my eyes: tappet of water against the boat, sound of an Anasazi's six-hole flute. And I watch the bank for beaver tracks, for any movement.

The canyon seems like a grandfather.

ONE EVENING, Winter and perhaps half the group carry instruments and recording gear back into Blacktail Canyon to a spot sound engineer Mickey Houlihan says is good for recording.

Winter likes to quote from Thoreau: "The woods would be very silent if no birds sang except those that sing best." The remark seems not only to underscore the ephemeral nature of human evolution but the necessity in evaluating any phenomenon—a canyon, a life, a song—of providing for change.

After several improvisations dominated by a cappella voice and percussion, Winter asks Larry Roark to try something on the euphonium; he and Rumbel and Darling will then come up around him. Roark is silent. Moonlight glows on the canyon's lips. There is the sound of gurgling water. After a word of encouragement, feeling shrouded in anonymous darkness like the rest of us, Larry puts his mouth to the horn.

For a while he is alone. God knows what visions of waterfalls or wrens, of boats in the rapids, of Bach or Mozart, are in his head, in his fingers, to send forth notes. The whine of the soprano sax finds him. And the flutter of the oboe. And the rumbling of the choral cello. The exchange lasts perhaps twenty minutes. Furious and sweet, anxious, rolling, delicate and raw. The last six or eight hanging notes are Larry's. Then there is a long silence. Winter finally says, "My God."

I feel, sitting in the wet dark in bathing suit and sneakers and T-shirt, that my fingers have brushed one of life's deep, coursing threads. Like so much else in the canyon, it is left alone. Speak, even notice it, and it would disappear.

I had come to the canyon with expectations. I had

wanted to see snowy egrets flying against the black schist at dusk; I saw blue-winged teal against the deep green waters at dawn. I had wanted to hear thunder rolling in the thousand-foot depths; I heard Winter's soprano sax resonating in Matkatameba Canyon, with the guttural caws of four ravens which circled above him. I had wanted to watch rattlesnakes; I saw in an abandoned copper mine, in the beam of my flashlight, a wall of copper sulphate that looked like a wall of turquoise. I rose each morning at dawn and washed in the cold river. I went to sleep each night listening to the cicadas, the pencil-ticking sound of some other insect, the soughing of river waves in tamarisk roots, and watching bats plunge and turn, looking like leaves blown around against the sky. What any of us had come to see or do fell away. We found ourselves at each turn with what we had not imagined.

THE LAST EVENING IT RAINED. We had left the canyon and been carried far out onto Lake Mead by the river's current. But we stood staring backward, at the point where the canyon had so obviously and abruptly ended.

A thought that stayed with me was that I had entered a private place in the earth. I had seen exposed nearly its oldest part. I had lost my sense of urgency, rekindled a sense of what people were, clambering to gain access to high waterfalls where we washed our hair together; and a sense of our endless struggle as a species to understand time and to estimate the consequences of our acts.

It rained the last evening. But before it did, Nancy Rumbel moved to the highest point on Scorpion Island in Lake Mead and played her oboe before a storm we could see hanging over Nevada. Sterling Smyth, who would return to programming computers in twenty-four hours, created a twelve-string imitation of the canyon wren, a long guitar solo. David Darling, revealed suddenly stark, again and then again, against a white-lightning sky, bowed furious homage to the now overhanging cumulonimbus.

In the morning we touched the far shore of Lake Mead, boarded a bus and headed for the Las Vegas airport. We were still wrapped in the journey, as though it were a Navajo blanket. We departed on various planes and arrived home in various cities and towns and at some point the world entered again and the hardest thing, the translation of what we had touched, began.

I sat in the airport in San Francisco, waiting for a connecting flight to Oregon, dwelling on one image. At the mouth of Nankoweap Canyon, the river makes a broad turn, and it is possible to see high in the orange rock what seem to be four small windows. They are entrances to granaries, built by the Anasazi who dwelled in the canyon a thousand years ago. This was provision against famine, to ensure the people would survive.

I do not know, really, how we will survive without places like the Inner Gorge of the Grand Canyon to visit. Once in a lifetime, even, is enough. To feel the stripping down, an ebb of the press of conventional time, a radical change of proportion, an unspoken respect for others that elicits keen emotional pleasure, a quick, intimate pounding of the heart.

Some parts of the trip will emerge one day on an album. Others will be found in a gesture of friendship to some stranger in an airport, in a letter of outrage to a planner of dams, in a note of gratitude to nameless faces in the Park Service, in wondering at the relatives of the ubiquitous wren, in the belief, passed on in whatever fashion—a photograph, a chord, a sketch—that nature can heal.

The living of life, any life, involves great and private pain, much of which we share with no one. In such places as the Inner Gorge the pain trails away from us. It is not so quiet there or so removed that you can hear yourself think, that you would even wish to; that comes later. You can hear your heart beat. That comes first.

# Trying the Land

ON WINTER AFTERNOONS Richard and I cross through the woods behind the farm he rents, cross the long pasture where the white horse remains distant (wild mustard coming in strong here, come spring), and slip into the farther country along the creek, like salmon. The days are overcast and wet. We go miles without speaking.

Richard hands me a black cottonwood leaf that covers both my hands, and goes on. I examine it, expertly. The detritus of the forest floor that clings to it; the patches of disintegration where the gossamer veinery is exposed, like steel rods uncovered in a roadbed.

Two snails, barely visible, small as pinheads, chew at the leaf. Snails at work, tearing the woods apart.

We cast about for the dogs. Gone ahead somewhere.

In the creek flats the alder is thick as row corn, and the signs of beaver are everywhere. We come to a skidway where they have cut and hauled, moved this fodder down to the bank, then off to deep water to anchor it against the hard months.

And here, deep in the woods, we find a huge ash, big enough and straight enough to floor my house four times over. But we aren't beaver. Or we care too much for such secrets, and move on.

The down Douglas fir that used to take us across at the mouth of the creek is gone, blown out in high water in a country without dams, hurled end for end into the river (which is dammed, higher up, and so in summer a damned liar whose water level makes no sense).

We find a way across, get wet, and have to help both dogs. They get on well in the woods. Are quiet. I trust when we spook deer that they will heel. Years ago I would have eaten meat brought to bay by dogs. Now I take the meat straight across or not at all. Each year these contracts with game animals are renewed, rewritten. Each year you grow older and there are new terms.

On the other side we come on a beaver dam and a lodge. We imagine them in there, imagining us, and go on after moments of appreciation. More than moments: I am on my knees, inspecting the intricate levelheadedness of the dam, touching the mystery. The dogs stand quiet as seals in the still water. I tell Richard: There is a line in Maximilian of Weid's journal—"We saw white wolves on the opposite shore, and the cranes flew heavily before us." Richard, a woodworker, reads as much as I do. We trade a good many books in winter. And I speak of Maximilian, who came up the Missouri River with the painter Karl Bodmer in 1832, often, as though he were a relative.

ABOVE THE BEAVER POND we find a trap. No. 4 Newhouse. Bread-and-butter beaver trap in the 1850s, and still around. Designed by Sewell Newhouse, resident at the Oneida Community in New York after 1849. Newhouse wanted trapping and his traps to spread like gospel in the wilderness. In 1869 he wrote in *The Trapper's Guide* that his trap, "going before the axe and the plow, forms the prow with which iron-clad civilization is pushing back barbaric solitude; causing the bear and the beaver to give place to the wheatfield, the library and the piano."

The trap was sprung years ago and forgotten. I don't mention Sewell to Richard, gone ahead. I follow his tracks and the dogs' (my wet, cold hands buried in my pants pockets) trying to remember the afternoon when I was nineteen and clearing trails in the Teton National Forest with an old man named Bill Daniels, who jumped suddenly off his horse and ran to the foot of a tree where, cursing the loss of memory, he dug up a bear trap he'd set in 1921: unsprung. No. 6 Newhouse. Rusted open. Big enough to trap a truck tire. Walking with my hands in my pockets (recalling the morning I slipped off a log's frosty back and ripped the pockets out of my parka trying to get my hands free to break the fall, and didn't make it).

The woods are soaked Pacific Northwest Douglas fir–dominated rain forest. Eighty inches of rain a year here. When David Douglas came into this country in 1825 his backers in London at the Horticultural Society thought his was a long shot to bring back to Europe the first collection of Pacific Northwest flora. Slight of build, chronically shy, he was determined, exact, and as self-contained in the woods as mercury. The Indians thought highly of him, took him to see the fabled sugar pines with cones as long as a man's arm from elbow to knuckles. When I walk in the woods in winter, damp but warm in wool clothes, I think of him huddled over his fire each evening hand-drying each of the day's specimens to preserve them—just as a man who fell in a creek might hold his notes up to the sun to dry them, that earnest. When Douglas returned to London in 1827 his herbarium became the celebration of English naturalists. His second trip, farther north, fared as well until the whole collection went to the bottom of the Fraser River in a nameless rapids, as quick as popping a button on a shirt.

RICHARD IS WAITING at a rock outcrop. We back up like bears into a shallow cave and eat, watching the woods, listening for spruce grouse. The dogs sleep.

Richard is the only man I know who's read all of Samuel Pepys.

In the cave there are certain mysteries—the presence of an animal once here (last winter?)—no sign of which can I finally discover. But I enjoy the sense of certainty. I look up to find both dogs staring at me.

We step back into the woods and turn upslope for the ridge. We climb, our hair damp with rain, our foreheads beaded with sweat, breathing like bulls. John Muir, God, how you went on, as detached as a raven, alone, barely provisioned, as indomitable as a wolverine in those Sierra snows, to find the winter life of the water ouzel. The bird remains largely unknown now, sixty years after you're dead and gone, and your ashes scattered. We reach the top, blowing like whales, unable to see anything in the fog.

I run my hands down the flanks of a slick-skinned madrone and wonder at all the things I think I've touched and haven't, while the fog condenses on the madrone where my fingers have passed.

In summer we've lain up here like wolves watching the country below for deer, after having eaten down there at the creek, yellow violets, sorrel and cress; like deer.

We come downslope as graceless as boulders.

Beneath a cover of barren alder branches at the creek's edge, in the failing light in our dark clothes, we hide. Still for a long time (the dogs, used to this, asleep back in the trees) before the birds come back. Mergansers skim the surface of the creek like skipped stones, headed upwater. That river monk, great blue heron, meditating behind the lightning strike of his beak in a downwater pool. Long moments and then we hear scream but do not see an osprey, who has seen us; and the heron lifts as slowly as a dirigible and evaporates downstream, and we go too.

We cross the creek at a familiar place and note without speaking the signs that others are using the same log-across-the-water crossing. Raccoon. Deer. High fast winter water. Working back south along the creek we are whipped hard by the leafless vine maple, cracked in the shins as though the loss of leaves had made them angry and they cared not a damn for the plot of seasons. Vine maple and I do not get on well, winter or summer.

Muir, do you know we cut the same country, that our walks are just shorter now? (Once in Livingston, Montana, a harmless drunken cowboy hung over me and demanded to know what it was I was reading, and I, young, said just a novel and quickly stuck it away in my things. It was George Catlin's journal. I was seduced by firsthand reports.)

Richard reaches down ahead of me, snaps up a deer's small pelvis, and waves his find (smooth, cool as marble), slips it into his shirt.

The light is going fast. We are always caught like this at dusk, and must break cross-country by dead reckoning past towering cedars at a constant pace to get to the road. On the way I spot grouse flowers, tight against the earth. First sign of spring.

# Landscape and Narrative

ONE SUMMER EVENING in a remote village in the Brooks Range of Alaska, I sat among a group of men listening to hunting stories about the trapping and pursuit of animals. I was particularly interested in several incidents involving wolverine, in part because a friend of mine was studying wolverine in Canada, among the Cree, but, too, because I find this animal such an intense creature. To hear about its life is to learn more about fierceness.

Wolverines are not intentionally secretive, hiding their lives from view, but they are seldom observed. The range of their known behavior is less than that of, say, bears or wolves. Still, that evening no gratuitous details were set out. This was somewhat odd, for wolverine easily excite the imagination; they can loom suddenly in the landscape with authority, with an aura larger than their compact physical dimensions, drawing one's immediate and complete attention. Wolverine also have a deserved reputation for resoluteness in the worst winters, for ferocious strength. But neither did these attributes induce the men to embellish.

I listened carefully to these stories, taking pleasure in the sharply observed detail surrounding the dramatic thread of events. The story I remember most vividly was about a man hunting a wolverine from a snow machine in the spring. He followed the animal's tracks for several miles over rolling tundra in a certain valley. Soon he caught sight ahead of a dark spot on the crest of a hill—the wolverine pausing to look back. The hunter was catching up, but each time he came over a rise the wolverine was looking back from the next rise, just out of range. The hunter topped one more rise and met the wolverine bounding toward him. Before he could pull his rifle from its scabbard the wolverine flew across the engine cowl and the windshield, hitting him square in the chest. The hunter scrambled his arms wildly, trying to get the wolverine out of his lap, and fell over as he did so. The wolverine jumped clear as the snow machine rolled over, and fixed the man with a stare. He had not bitten, not even scratched the man. Then the wolverine walked away. The man thought of reaching for the gun, but no, he did not.

The other stories were like this, not so much making a point as evoking something about contact with wild animals that would never be completely understood.

When the stories were over, four or five of us walked out of the home of our host. The surrounding land, in the persistent light of a far northern summer, was still visible for miles—the striated, pitched massifs of the Brooks Range; the shy, willow-lined banks of the John River flowing south from Anaktuvuk Pass; and the flat tundra plain, opening with great affirmation to the north. The landscape seemed alive because of the stories. It was precisely these ocherous tones, this kind of willow, exactly this austerity that had informed the wolverine narratives. I felt exhilaration, and a deeper confirmation of the stories. The mundane tasks which awaited me I anticipated now with pleasure. The stories had renewed in me a sense of the purpose of my life.

THIS FEELING, an inexplicable renewal of enthusiasm after storytelling, is familiar to many people. It does not seem to matter greatly what the subject is, as long as the context is intimate and the story is told for its own sake, not forced to serve merely as the vehicle for an idea. The tone of the story need not be solemn. The darker aspects of life need not be ignored. But I think intimacy is indispensable—a feeling that derives from the listener's trust and a storyteller's certain knowledge of his subject and regard for his audience. This intimacy deepens if the storyteller tempers his authority with humility, or when terms of idiomatic expression, or at least the physical setting for the story, are shared.

I think of two landscapes—one outside the self, the other within. The external landscape is the one we see—not only the line and color of the land and its shading at different times of the day, but also its plants and animals in season, its weather, its geology, the record of its climate and evolution. If you walk up, say, a dry arroyo in the Sonoran Desert you will feel a mounding and rolling of sand and silt beneath your foot that is distinctive. You will anticipate the crumbling of the sedimentary earth in the arroyo bank as your hand reaches out, and in that tangible evidence you will sense a history of water in the region. Perhaps a black-throated sparrow lands in a paloverde bush—the resiliency of the twig under the bird, that precise shade of yellowish-green against the milk-blue sky, the fluttering whir of the arriving sparrow, are what I mean by "the landscape." Draw on the smell of creosote bush, or clack stones together in the dry air. Feel how light is the desiccated dropping of the kangaroo rat. Study an animal track obscured by the wind. These are all elements of the land, and what makes the landscape comprehensible are the relationships between them. One learns a landscape finally not by knowing the name or identity of everything in it, but by perceiving the relationships in it—like that between the sparrow and the twig. The difference between the relationships and the elements is the same as that between written history and a catalog of events.

The second landscape I think of is an interior one, a kind of projection within a person of a part of the exterior landscape. Relationships in the exterior landscape include those that are named and discernible, such as the nitrogen cycle, or a vertical sequence of Ordovician limestone, and others that are uncodified or ineffable, such as winter light falling on a particular kind of granite, or the effect of humidity on the frequency of a blackpoll warbler's burst of song. That these relationships have purpose and order, however inscrutable they may seem to us, is a tenet of evolution. Similarly, the speculations, intuitions, and formal ideas we refer to as "mind" are a set of relationships in the interior landscape with purpose and order; some of these are obvious, many impenetrably subtle. The shape and character of these relationships in a person's thinking, I believe, are deeply influenced by where on this earth one goes, what one touches, the patterns one observes in nature—the intricate history of one's life in the land, even a life in the city, where wind, the chirp of birds, the line of a falling leaf, are known. These thoughts are arranged, further, according to the thread of one's moral, intellectual, and spiritual development. The interior landscape responds to the character and subtlety of an exterior landscape; the shape of the individual mind is affected by land as it is by genes.

In stories like those I heard at Anaktuvuk Pass

about wolverine, the relationship between separate elements in the land is set forth clearly. It is put in a simple framework of sequential incidents and apposite detail. If the exterior landscape is limned well, the listener often feels that he has heard something pleasing and authentic—trustworthy. We derive this sense of confidence I think not so much from verifiable truth as from an understanding that lying has played no role in the narrative. The storyteller is obligated to engage the reader with a precise vocabulary, to set forth a coherent and dramatic rendering of incidents—and to be ingenuous.

When one hears a story one takes pleasure in it for different reasons—for the euphony of its phrases, an aspect of the plot, or because one identifies with one of the characters. With certain stories certain individuals may experience a deeper, more profound sense of well-being. This latter phenomenon, in my understanding, rests at the heart of storytelling as an elevated experience among aboriginal peoples. It results from bringing two landscapes together. The exterior landscape is organized according to principles or laws or tendencies beyond human control. It is understood to contain an integrity that is beyond human analysis and unimpeachable. Insofar as the storyteller depicts various subtle and obvious relationships in the exterior landscape accurately in his story, and insofar as he orders them along traditional lines of meaning to create the narrative, the narrative will "ring true." The listener who "takes the story to heart" will feel a pervasive sense of congruence within himself and also with the world.

Among the Navajo and, as far as I know, many other native peoples, the land is thought to exhibit a sacred order. That order is the basis of ritual. The rituals themselves reveal the power in that order. Art, architecture, vocabulary, and costume, as well as ritual, are derived from the perceived natural order of the universe—from observations and meditations on the exterior landscape. An indigenous philosophy—metaphysics, ethics, epistemology, aesthetics, and logic—may also be derived from a people's continuous attentiveness to both the obvious (scientific) and ineffable (artistic) orders of the local landscape. Each individual, further, undertakes to order his interior landscape according to the exterior landscape. To succeed in this means to achieve a balanced state of mental health.

I think of the Navajo for a specific reason. Among the various sung ceremonies of this people—Enemyway, Coyoteway, Red Antway, Uglyway—is one called Beautyway. In the Navajo view, the elements of one's interior life—one's psychological makeup and moral bearing—are subject to a persistent principle of disarray. Beautyway is, in part, a spiritual invocation of the order of the exterior universe, that irreducible, holy complexity that manifests itself as all things changing through time (a Navajo definition of beauty, hózhǫ́ǫ́). The purpose of this invocation is to recreate in the individual who is the subject of the Beautyway ceremony that same order, to make the individual again a reflection of the myriad enduring relationships of the landscape.

I believe story functions in a similar way. A story

draws on relationships in the exterior landscape and projects them onto the interior landscape. The purpose of storytelling is to achieve harmony between the two landscapes, to use all the elements of story—syntax, mood, figures of speech—in a harmonious way to reproduce the harmony of the land in the individual's interior. Inherent in story is the power to reorder a state of psychological confusion through contact with the pervasive truth of those relationships we call "the land."

THESE THOUGHTS, of course, are susceptible to interpretation. I am convinced, however, that these observations can be applied to the kind of prose we call nonfiction as well as to traditional narrative forms such as the novel and the short story, and to some poems. Distinctions between fiction and nonfiction are sometimes obscured by arguments over what constitutes "the truth." In the aboriginal literature I am familiar with, the first distinction made among narratives is to separate the authentic from the inauthentic. Myth, which we tend to regard as fictitious or "merely metaphorical," is as authentic, as real, as the story of a wolverine in a man's lap. (A distinction is made, of course, about the elevated nature of myth—and frequently the circumstances of myth-telling are more rigorously prescribed than those for the telling of legends or vernacular stories—but all of these narratives are rooted in the local landscape. To violate *that* connection is to call the narrative itself into question.)

The power of narrative to nurture and heal, to repair a spirit in disarray, rests on two things: the skillful invocation of unimpeachable sources and a listener's knowledge that no hypocrisy or subterfuge is involved. This last simple fact is to me one of the most imposing aspects of the Holocene history of man.

We are more accustomed now to thinking of "the truth" as something that can be explicitly stated, rather than as something that can be evoked in a metaphorical way outside science and Occidental culture. Neither can truth be reduced to aphorism or formulas. It is something alive and unpronounceable. Story creates an atmosphere in which it becomes discernible as a pattern. For a storyteller to insist on relationships that do not exist is to lie. Lying is the opposite of story. (I do not mean to confuse ignorance with deception, or to imply that a storyteller can perceive all that is inherent in the land. Every storyteller falls short of a perfect limning of the landscape—perception and language both fail. But to make up something that is not there, something which can never be corroborated in the land, to knowingly set forth a false relationship, is to be lying, no longer telling a story.)

Because of the intricate, complex nature of the land, it is not always possible for a storyteller to grasp what is contained in a story. The intent of the storyteller, then, must be to evoke, honestly, some single aspect of all that the land contains. The storyteller knows that because different individuals grasp the story at different levels, the focus of his regard for truth must be at the primary one—with who was there, what happened, when, where, and why things occurred. The story will then possess similar truth at other levels—the integrity inherent at the primary level of meaning will be conveyed everywhere else. As long as the storyteller carefully describes the order before him, and uses his storytelling skill to heighten and emphasize certain relationships, it is even possible for the story to be more successful than the storyteller himself is able to imagine.

I WOULD LIKE TO MAKE a final point about the wolverine stories I heard at Anaktuvuk Pass. I wrote down the details afterward, concentrating especially on aspects of the biology and ecology of the animals. I sent the information on to my friend living with the Cree. When, many months later, I saw him, I asked whether the Cree had enjoyed these insights of the Nunamiut into the nature of the wolverine. What had they said?

"You know," he told me, "how they are. They said, 'That could happen.' "

In these uncomplicated words the Cree declared their own knowledge of the wolverine. They acknowledged that although they themselves had never seen the things the Nunamiut spoke of, they accepted them as accurate observations, because they did not consider story a context for misrepresentation. They also preserved their own dignity by not overstating their confidence in the Nunamiut, a distant and unknown people.

Whenever I think of this courtesy on the part of

the Cree I think of the dignity that is ours when we cease to demand the truth and realize that the best we can have of those substantial truths that guide our lives is metaphorical—a story. And the most of it we are likely to discern comes only when we accord one another the respect the Cree showed the Nunamiut. Beyond this—that the interior landscape is a metaphorical representation of the exterior landscape, that the truth reveals itself most fully not in dogma but in the paradox, irony, and contradictions that distinguish compelling narratives—beyond this there are only failures of imagination: reductionism in science; fundamentalism in religion; fascism in politics.

Our national literatures should be important to us insofar as they sustain us with illumination and heal us. They can always do that so long as they are written with respect for both the source and the reader, and with an understanding of why the human heart and the land have been brought together so regularly in human history.

# Yukon-Charley: The Shape of Wilderness

I KNOW THAT COCOON FEELING, wearing wool socks, long underwear, jeans, hip boots, several shirts, a down vest and windbreaker. Sitting motionless in the bow of the nineteen-foot Grumman as it cuts cold water transparent as glass, I imagine I can pull my skin back from the innermost wall of fabric, pretend that I have found, by some inexplicable and private adventure, the tunnel to a strange window: I look out on what the map calls the Eastern Intermontane Plateau physiographic province, deep in Alaska's gut. Some of the peaks in the distance have no names; the water of the Charley River rides like glycerin up my fingers and over my palm, feels frigid against my wrist.

Behind us, eight miles to the east, the Charley enters the upper Yukon. Sixty miles to the north, the Yukon will pass the town of Circle, from where we have come. Another sixty miles farther on, at Fort Yukon, the Porcupine will come in. Then the Yukon will turn sharply southwest and line out a thousand riverine miles to Norton Sound and the Bering Sea. From this cartographer's sense of isolation, as though I had vibrissae or other antennae extended, I surface, aware we will hit the gravel bar ahead, haul out, and build a fire to cook, to dry socks soaked in leaky boots.

I look up, as if drawn by puppet strings, to find a bald eagle dipping its hunting arc over us. Working the river. It breaks away and heads north and west into low mountains. The bow of the canoe rides up hard, rattling over the stones.

It is hours between such noises.

On shore we find again what we have known with such pleasure for days—signs of animals. Fresh moose tracks, much older bear tracks, and the bones of a grayling from some animal's meal. With 10 x 40 Leitz glasses, elbows pressed to my knees, I can see back down the river: warbonnet heads of red-breasted mergansers, long-necked pintails, the green bandit masks of male widgeon, and white, quarter-moon slashes on the faces of male blue-winged teal. Some of the birds are so far away I have to guess.

Our trip had begun that morning from a base camp

on a gravel bar in the middle of the Yukon at the mouth of the Charley. The Charley's luminous black surface, crinkling in the wind, foundered in the silt-laden, war-horse current of the larger river, as far across as a Dakota wheat field, a bold child slipping into a twilight clearing.

The first morning in camp on the Yukon we found fresh grizzly tracks only twenty feet from the tent, an errand that, thankfully, hadn't included us. In the benign light of an arctic summer—the two of us stood about, waking up with mugs of coffee, our shoulders to a cool wind—a beaver arrived. Huge, he slacked his stroke, circling back in the leaden sweep of the river, slapped his tail twice and moved on, his head riding the current like the bow bumper of a tugboat. I watched a marsh hawk alone far to the west, a harrier, unload itself repeatedly against the wind in somersaults and chandelles and remembered the erroneous summary of the field guide: ". . . the flight low, languid, and gliding." He flew as if his name were unrecorded.

That morning, too, as I pulled on my boots, a wolverine walked into camp, looked us over, stabbing the air with his nose to confirm what he saw: dead end. Bob and I stood up, as though someone important had walked in, his arrival as unexpected as the smell of cinnamon.

THE CHARLEY and the Yukon, the beaver, the widgeon, the grizzly, lie within a federal preserve, created by emergency presidential order under provisions of the Antiquities Act and designated Yukon-Charley Rivers National Preserve on December 2, 1980. Among the reasons for this laying by: an exemplary weaving of interior Alaska flora and fauna. Untouched by Ice Age glaciation, the land has a high potential as a reservoir for undisturbed early aboriginal sites. The area is rich in fur-trapping and gold-mining history. And it offers protection for an entire watershed, that of the Charley, and for peregrine falcons, who nest on the high bluffs that rise along this part of the upper Yukon.

The landscape itself, however, the pattern of birch and spruce and creeks spreading over the hills and up into the steep mountains where sheep dwell, shows no sign of the designation. There are no green park buildings, no managers, campfire circles or roads. Instead there is the trace evidence of thirty or so people living here, placer miners and subsistence trappers whose predecessors have been in the vicinity for more than eighty years. Their cabins are spotted every six or seven miles along the Yukon; the colored floats on gill nets bob close by on the khaki-brown surface of the river—salmon nets, winter food for their dogs. At Coal Creek and Woodchopper Creek, the two working mines, crude landing strips have been bulldozed near a few buildings; the mills and the rest of the improbable heavy machinery were brought into the country by barge. Supplies come to this part of the river now by skiff, canoe, dogsled, or snow machine, depending on the season and one's circumstances, down from the roadhead at Eagle,

105 miles above the mouth of the Charley, or up from Circle.

Until someone forces them to change their way of life, to give all this up and quit the country, the Yukon-Charley Rivers National Preserve will, in residents' minds, remain little more than a colored panel on someone else's map. The formal setting aside of this land, in fact, represents to them an incomplete understanding of the country.

WHEN WE SHOVED OFF from camp that morning on the Yukon we took most of our gear in the canoe with us, a nuisance, but a necessary precaution against bears, who might shred it or drag it off into the river.

The sight of the broad back of the Yukon in mid-June triggers a memory of the Nile or the Amazon; but breakup ice is piled in shattered rafts the size of freight cars along the shores. The banks have been deeply gouged, the bark scraped from trees to reveal gleaming yellow-white flesh beneath. Silt boils against the canoe, a white noise that is with us until we cross half a mile of open water and hit the Charley. Its transparent flow, turned against the downstream bank of the bigger river, narrows to nothing after a thousand yards, absorbed.

The mouth of the Charley—its name oddly prosaic, a miner's notion, fitting the human history of the region—is a good place to fish for pike or burbot. (We bait a trotline for burbot, a freshwater cod that looks like a catfish. We will check it on the way out.) The flats of the river's floodplain, several square miles, are dense with an even growth of willow, six to eight feet high. The undersides of the long, narrow leaves are a lighter shade of green than that above; their constant movement, a synaptic fury in the wind, makes them seem all the more luminous. Moose are bedded down among them, beyond the reach of our senses. Their tracks say so.

The river's banks, flooded with an aureate storm light underneath banks of nimbus cloud, are bright enough to astonish us—or me at least. My companion's attention is divided—the direction of the canoe, the stream of clues that engage a wildlife biologist: the height at which these willows have been browsed, the number of raven nests in that cliff, a torn primary feather which reaches us like a dry leaf on the surface of the water. Canada goose.

What is stunning about the river's banks on this particular stormy afternoon is not the vegetation (the willow, alder, birch, black cottonwood, and spruce are common enough) but its *presentation*. The wind, like some energetic dealer in rare fabrics, folds back branches and ruffles the underside of leaves to show the pattern—the shorter willows forward; the birch, taller, set farther back on the hills. The soft green furze of budding alder heightens the contrast between gray-green willow stems and white birch bark. All of it is rhythmic in the wind, each species bending as its diameter, its surface area, the strength of its fibers dictate. Behind this, a backdrop of hills: open country recovering from an old fire, dark islands of spruce in an ocean of labrador tea, lowbush cranberry, fireweed, and wild primrose, each species of leaf the invention of a different green: lime, moss, forest, jade. This is not to mention the steel gray of the clouds, the balmy arctic temperature, our clear suspension in the canoe over the stony floor of the river, the ground-in dirt of my hands, the flutelike notes of a Swainson's thrush, or anything else that informs the scene.

A local trapper advised us against the Charley. Too common, too bleak. Try the Kandick, he said, farther up the Yukon. I did not see a way in the conversation—it was too short, too direct—to convey my pleasure before mere color, the artifices of the wind. My companion and I exchanged a discreet shrug as we left the man's cabin. Differing views of what will excite the traveler.

At Bonanza Creek, while our socks dried by the fire, we fished for arctic grayling. Our plan had been to go twenty-five or thirty miles farther up the Charley, to where mountains rise precipitously on both sides and we might see Dall sheep with their lambs, or even spot a new species of butterfly (a lepidopterist in Fairbanks, learning of our destination, had urged a collecting kit on each of us). We abandoned the plan. Mosquitoes got to us as the river narrowed, and it was a banner year for them. Step a few feet into the bush and hundreds were on you. Insect repellant only kept them from biting—

and they quickly found any unsprayed spot where cloth hugged skin close enough to let them drive home, so often the inside of a thigh. Nothing to be done about their whining madly in the ears, clogging the throat, clouding one's vision.

The memory of our windswept campsite on the Yukon, far from shore, a gravel bar without vegetation and so mosquito-free, passed wordlessly between us. We put on dry socks, cleaned two grayling, folded our 1:250,000 physiographic maps, and swung the Grumman downriver.

IN THE SUMMER OF 1967 grizzly bears killed two people in Glacier National Park. The Park Service killed the bears and ignited a controversy about the meaning and importance of wilderness in America. The timber industry, for its part, said wilderness was the private playground of a young, upper-middle-class elite. This castigation obscured their own considerable peevishness: according to the prevailing federal mandate—to seek to manage public lands for recreation, logging, grazing, mining, hunting, fishing, and watershed protection—wilderness failed to serve only logging.

An argument for wilderness that reaches beyond the valid concerns of multiple-use—recreation, flood control, providing a source of pure water—is that wild lands preserve complex biological relationships that we are only dimly, or sometimes not at all, aware of. Wilderness represents a gene pool, vital for the resiliency of plants and animals. An argument for wilderness that goes deeper still is that we have an ethical obligation to provide animals with a place where they are free from the impingements of civilization. And, further, an historical responsibility to preserve the kind of landscapes from which modern man emerged.

The Reagan administration regards such arguments as these from science and ethics as frivolous. It wishes to reduce "the wilderness controversy" to economic terms, which is like trying to approach the collapse of a national literature as primarily an economic problem. The administration's attitude reveals an impoverished understanding of the place and history of the physical landscape in human affairs—of its effect, for example, on the evolution and structure of language, or on the development of particular regional literatures, even on the ontogeny of human personalities. Such observations have been offered by writers and artists recently to make a single point: as vital as any single rationale for the preservation of undisturbed landscapes is regard for the profound effect they can have on the direction of human life.

The insistence of government and industry, that wilderness values be rendered solely in economic terms, has led to an insidious presumption, that the recreational potential of wild land, not its biological integrity, should be the principal criterion of its worth. This, in turn, has shifted public attention away from concerns about wilderness that are harder to define (or price out) and created problems of its own, by making personal risk and physical exertion more the hallmarks of a wilderness experience than finding humility and serenity. The spiritual, aesthetic, and historical dimensions of wilderness experience, at least in congressional hearings, have become subordinate.

Wilderness travel can be extremely taxing and dangerous. You can fall into a crevasse, flip your kayak, lose your way, become hypothermic, run out of food, or be killed by a bear. Far less violent events, however, are the common experience of most people who travel in wild landscapes. A sublime encounter with perhaps the most essential attribute of wilderness—falling into resonance with a system of unmanaged, non-human-centered relationships—can be as fulfilling as running a huge and difficult rapid. Sometimes they prove, indeed, to be the same thing.

America, at least in its written law, is uncertain what it values in wilderness, beyond recreational utility. Some who might succinctly address the larger issues—child psychiatrists, geneticists, theologians—don't view themselves as spokesmen. That wilderness can revitalize someone who has spent too long in the highly manipulative, perversely efficient atmosphere of modern life is a widely shared notion; but whether wilderness experience has a clear therapeutic value remains scientifically uncertain.

These more subtle arguments for the preservation of wilderness point directly to our ethical and psychological well-being as a country. Though they lag light-years behind in having any legal standing they are as critical as economic arguments and much of this suggests that the real wisdom of the Wilderness Act of 1964, setting wilderness aside, has yet to fully emerge.

AGAINST THE BACKDROP of such lofty thoughts the Yukon-Charley Rivers National Preserve seems somewhat anomalous because it lacks spectacle. Set for comparison against the Valhalla of Denali National Park or the Cambrian silence of Grand Canyon it seems commonplace. But for the presence of relatively numerous peregrines, its river headlands differ little from those along the Hudson, pleasing but not distinguished. Its hills remind one of the Blue Ridge, a reclining countryside. The Yukon itself at this point is without rapids or picturesque waterfalls and thick with silt. In the spring of 1981 there was also a general scarcity of large animals. There is nothing at all, in fact, very remarkable about the place—except that it is largely uninhabited and undisturbed. That people live here is unusual. Theoretically their presence is to be regarded as a drawback to wilderness, though they actually give the land a pleasing dimension.

The loss of animals is puzzling. There is a curiously persistent popular belief that if wild animals are left alone they will flourish in wilderness areas and reach an "optimum population" in balance with other species in the ecosystem; but this is not so. Like any other landscape, the Yukon-Charley country is susceptible to forest fires, hard winters, epizootic disease, and predator pressure. It has had good as well as lean years; no one knows enough wildlife biology to determine precisely why recent years have been ones in which the populations of moose, wolverine, caribou, marten, bear, and wolf have dwindled. The hunting pressure from outside the region has been fierce, and it is partly to blame; but the situation is as complicated a subject as schizophrenia or genetic drift. A visitor is not unwarranted, therefore, in speculating that the recent demise of animals may in some way be tied to the intense and proprietary scrutiny that the land has been subjected to—I sense the imposition of analytic thought, the imputation of logic on this guileless land, in my own notebook.

ONE MORNING on the Yukon we had to grit our teeth against a driving rainstorm. We put into shore when it showed no sign of letting up, only to be driven out by mosquitoes. We shoved off, wrapped in raingear, feeling the edge of that depression that comes with relentless bad weather. Two hours later we arrived at a place identified as a cabin on the map. Shelter, we thought. It would likely be a trapper's unoccupied winter residence, bearing a familiar notice—use it as your own, leave it as you found it.

The cabin reveals itself as a trapper's cabin but there is another kind of sign here, in store-bought, iridescent pink on black: PRIVATE PROPERTY, NO TRESPASSING. And on brown cardboard in hand-lettered black: OUR HOME IS PROTECTED WITH SET GUNS.

So does wild country change. There probably are no set guns, but we are not eager to test the idea. What the sign says is: *The country is filling up with people. I came here to get away from you. I'm not a backwoods nut shooting at peregrines. I don't own a bulldozer or contemplate building roads or condominiums and I don't pose a threat to anyone's peace of mind. This part of the nation's heritage will do just fine without any wilderness boundaries, without any rangers, or any tourists. Get lost.*

I understand, I think, the position. It's a gulf that divides old-guard Alaskans from those with urban concerns and perceptions. But I bear the man ill will in the pouring rain and swarming mosquitoes. There's not been this kind of rancor, this level of belligerence in the country before.

An hour later the rain stops. We haul up on a gravel bar, beneath a sun that grows brighter and hotter. For the next few hours we sleep sprawled on the warm stones while our equipment dries, then we eat, bail the canoe, and set up the spotting scope to watch a nest of young ravens on the opposite shore. Gulls swivel above, acrobatic in the blustery winds. Which are they? Without a bird guide we depend on each other to know, but are not distressed at forgetting the distinction between herring and mew gulls. We will look it up later. For now it is enough to be resting here in the streaming light.

I am drawn later to the water's edge, a primal attraction. Bent over like a heron I start upriver, searching for stones, lured by the sparkling quartzes and smooth bits of glistening debris: maroon and blue, wheat colors, speckled birds' eggs colors, purple, coal—I can settle twenty on the back of my hand, each one a different shade. I could poke here until I dropped of old age. My pockets slowly fill with stones, each tied vaguely to pleasure. It's ten-thirty at night. The sun, low on the northwest horizon, throws light across to a full moon in the southeast sky.

We fall asleep to a clatter of sandhill cranes, the running screech of a belted kingfisher. A breeze brings the spermish odor of balsam poplars over the water to lie punk in our noses.

On the river the following day, the rain squalls behind us, I wonder about violence in a place like this. A caribou cow swatted to its knees by a bear. Lightning-caused fires rage out of control twenty miles north of us in an unnamed valley. Frozen lenses of underground ice leer like a dark Norwegian secret from beneath the brows of the river's banks. A peregrine snatches a teal from the sky like a paper bag. A cow moose, driven mad by insects in her face, thrashes in willows. A wolf carcass lies rotting on the shore. The images whisper to me of the fullness of the land, of the tentativeness of my visit.

In search of water free of silt we turn up Sam Creek. Flocks of goldeneye with their high foreheads explode vertically off its tannin-colored waters. Mallards sweep past and arctic loons labor by, dipnecked and humpbacked like seals. It's as though we had barged in. Thousands of multicolored feathers float amid stalks of horsetail fern at the creek's edge. Snagged on one of the scabrous sheaths is the hooked, iridescent tail feather of a male mallard. My hands are slick with river silt, stiffened by wind and sun. I can hardly grasp it.

WE OFTEN COME TO WILDERNESS to find animals; we are less sure about the presence of people. In the Wilderness Act humans are construed as aliens, urged to make their visits relatively brief and to leave no mark of their passage. There are good reasons for this. Some people, oblivious to any but their own needs, leave a bright spoor; others have a resident's instincts and wish to build corrals and emergency shelters in country they visit regularly. But there is something unsettling in this kind of purity. To banish all evidence of ourselves means the wilderness is to that extent contrived. We are not, in fact, aliens; and Yukon-Charley offers a chance to reconsider this aspect of wilderness, and better determine what we mean by "human disturbance" in such places.

There are a handful of miners in Yukon-Charley. Under the present law they are allowed to stay on and work their claims. Resident subsistence hunters, who have expressed a desire to stay on but whose way of life is seen to be less responsible, less defensible than the gainfully employed miners', have been urged to go. These latter lives are ones of humble scale. To allow them to remain here, to go on working as indigenous guides, as translators of this experience for the rest of us, infrequent visitors, is an attractive thought. Such a life speaks to a need many of us have but few can attend to—long-lived intimacy with a place, being able to speak of it knowledgeably to others.

Such people, of course, would have to kill the local animals to feed themselves, and take fish from the river for their dogs. They would run trap lines. Perhaps it would never do. But if it could be people like the Moore family living on Sam Creek it would be worth it. To let them stay and hunt and speak with us would mean we would have rid ourselves of some abnegation.

The Moores have been living in Yukon-Charley for almost four years. George traps mink, marten, lynx, and wolverine and trades the furs for staples, clothing, and personal items. He and his wife, Kelly, both in their early thirties, have an infant son, Zachariah. They are congenial, alert, resourceful. They share everything they have with us—food, time, conversation, books. When George says quietly after dinner, "I want for nothing," the self-knowledge, the self-confidence in his words, has a ten-winter ring.

The Moores live a life many have tried and abandoned. They husband the scraps of the animals they hunt and trap, and put them to use in some way or other. From the furs they realize a small cash income. Their world, from what I saw, is not haunted by imaginary enemies. They are not hamstrung by schedules. Like the Athabascans in this country before them, they have a manifestly spiritual relationship with the landscape. Considering the physical labor and the harsh climate, their stamina and their belief in themselves are remarkable. To chance on them was to hear of the subtleties of making a living here, to have a history, to sense one's own visit against other years, other seasons.

In the face of such lives, one feels villainous, a coward, agreeing to a proposed federal order that would one day tell them to leave. It is shameful enough to want to kick them out; what is more distressing is that we have made this mistake before. We told the native peoples of North America that their relationships with the land were worthless, primitive. Now we are a culture that spends millions trying to find this knowledge, trying to reestablish a sense of well-being with the earth.

I would not argue with the need to preserve a wilderness free of human enterprise, but I would not want to be the one, if it came to their leaving, to explain the official reasoning to George Moore.

WE BROKE CAMP at the mouth of the Charley River late one afternoon and the Yukon drew us north toward Circle. The aluminum canoe revolved slowly in the current. We reached out with a paddle only to fend off trees torn loose in breakup or to negotiate fast water at the foot of a bluff.

This is remote wilderness, not apt to draw many visitors. Mosquitoes swarm in the summer and the days of winter are short, brutally cold. For all its undistinguished square miles, however, it is a good place to have set aside. Migratory birds by the hundreds of thousands find sustenance here, spring and fall. It is a country that allows bears room enough to hunt moose, and it provides fox ptarmigan enough to get through the winter. It casts up mile after mile of small, beautiful stones on its river banks; and its cliffs support endangered peregrines that range to Oklahoma and Mexico. Its air is laced with the sweet odor of balsam and the honk of geese, and its meadows burst in spring with clusters of bluebells and white-headed cotton grass, with the evaporating pinks of primroses, the camellia-like blossoms of bunchberry, the soft purple of wild gentian, and red bundles of the fireweed's blossoms. Its green hills stretch back easily from the river.

It is the sort of ordinary place that shaped many people in rural America. It is straightforward country that drives home two lessons. People who do come here will find, on looking, a mix of color, of smells, of events, that can be found nowhere else in the world. So the country, finally, is exceptional. And the profound elevation of the spirit in a wild place, rejuvenation, does not always require a rush of adrenaline. Sometimes lingering in a country's unpretentious hills and waters offers all one might wish of wisdom.

Somewhere down the Yukon, king salmon were coming. In a month dog salmon will follow. After them, after freeze-up, silver salmon. In some way each species will contrive to see in the dense, brown water, to smell, to clear its gills in order to breathe. They will nourish grizzly bears and subsistence families like the

Moores. Wolverines and bald eagles will scavenge their carcasses. Pike will eat their young.

In the low evening light stands of birch become dazzling rivers of white light, pouring down the hills of dark spruce. The bulbous ground shadows of cumulus clouds glide silently over distant slopes.

I remember an erratic wind blowing white blossoms off Kelly Moore's tomato plants; the *pas retiré* of willows; the abalone nacre in a dragonfly's back. And sensing one afternoon at the edge of a thick stand of spruce, drawn by a commotion of ravens, that we were suddenly too close, much too close, to a fresh bear kill. And how that wolverine *had just appeared in camp* while I was pulling on my boots.

THE LAST NIGHT ON THE RIVER we unroll goose-down bags on a tarpaulin thrown down over river sand and small stones. We do not speak of anything we have seen. We each wish in our different ways for some insurance against the disappearance of wild relationships here. These dreams of preservation for the very things that induce a sense of worth in human beings must have been dreamt seven thousand years ago on the Euphrates. They are dreams one hopes are dreamt on the Potomac but suspects may not be, dreams of respectful human participation in a landscape, generation after generation. Dreams of need and fulfillment. Common enough dreams. Poignant, ineffable, indefensible, the winds of an interior landscape. A handful of beautiful damp stones in arctic sunlight, a green duck feather stuck to one finger. Water dripping back to the river. I fumble at some prayer here I have forgotten, utterly forgotten, how to perform. I place the stones back in the river, as carefully as possible, and move inland to sleep.

# Borders

IN EARLY SEPTEMBER, the eastern Arctic coast of Alaska shows several faces, most of them harsh. But there are days when the wind drops and the sky is clear, and for reasons too fragile to explain—the overflight of thousands of migrating ducks, the bright, silent austerity of the Romanzof Mountains under fresh snow, the glassy stillness of the ocean—these days have an edge like no others. The dawn of such a clear and windless day is cherished against memories of late August snow squalls and days of work in rough water under leaden skies.

One such morning, a few of us on a biological

survey in the Beaufort Sea set that work aside with hardly a word and headed east over the water for the international border, where the state of Alaska abuts the Yukon Territory. The fine weather encouraged this bit of adventure.

There are no settlements along this part of the arctic coast. We did not in fact know if the border we were headed to was even marked. A northeast wind that had been driving loose pack ice close to shore for several days forced us to run near the beach in a narrow band of open water. In the lee of larger pieces of sea ice, the ocean had begun to freeze, in spite of the strong sunlight and a benign feeling in the air. Signs of winter.

As we drove toward Canada, banking the open, twenty-foot boat in graceful arcs to avoid pieces of drift ice, we hung our heads far back to watch migrating Canada geese and black brant pass over. Rifling past us and headed west at fifty miles an hour a foot off the water were flocks of oldsquaw, twenty and thirty ducks at a time. Occasionally, at the edge of the seaward ice, the charcoal-gray snout of a ringed seal would break the calm surface of the ocean for breath.

We drew nearer the border, wondering aloud how we would know it. I remembered a conversation of years before, with a man who had escaped from Czechoslovakia to come to America and had later paddled a canoe the length of the Yukon. He described the border where the river crossed into Alaska as marked by a great swath cut through the spruce forest. In the middle of nowhere, I said ruefully; what a waste of trees, how ugly it must have seemed. He looked silently across the restaurant table at me and said it was the easiest border crossing of his life.

I thought, as we drove on east, the ice closing in more now, forcing us to run yet closer to the beach, of the geographer Carl Sauer and his concept of biologically distinct regions. The idea of bioregionalism, as it has been developed by his followers, is a political concept that would reshape human life. It would decentralize residents of an area into smaller, more self-sufficient, environmentally responsible units, occupying lands the borders of which would be identical with the borders of natural regions—watersheds, for example. I thought of Sauer because we were headed that day for a great, invisible political dividing line: 141 degrees western longitude. Like the border between Utah and Colorado, this one is arbitrary. If it were not actually marked—staked—it would not be discernible. Sauer's borders are noticeable. Even the birds find them.

On the shore to our right, as we neared the mouth of Demarcation Bay, we saw the fallen remains of an Eskimo sod house, its meat-drying racks, made of driftwood, leaning askew. Someone who had once come this far to hunt had built the house. The house eventually became a dot on U.S. Coast and Geodetic Survey maps. Now its location is vital to the Inuit, for it establishes a politically important right of prior use, predating the establishment of the Arctic National Wildlife Refuge, within whose borders it has been included. I recall all this as we pass, from poring over our detailed maps the night before. Now, with the warmth of sunlight on the side of my face, with boyhood thoughts of the Yukon Territory welling up inside, the nearness of friends, with whom work has been such keen satisfaction these past few weeks, I have no desire to see maps.

Ahead, it is becoming clear that the closing ice is going to force us right up on the beach before long. The wedge of open water is narrowing. What there is is very still, skimmed with fresh slush ice. I think suddenly of my brother, who lives in a house on Block Island, off the coast of Rhode Island. When I visit we walk and drive around the island. Each time I mean to ask him, does he feel any more ordered in his life for being able to see so clearly the boundary between the ocean and the land in every direction? But I am never able to phrase the question right. And the old and dour faces of the resident islanders discourage it.

Far ahead, through a pair of ten-power binoculars, I finally see what appears to be a rampart of logs, weathered gray-white and standing on a bluff where the tundra falls off fifteen or twenty feet to the beach. Is this the border?

We are breaking ice now with the boat. At five miles an hour, the bow wave skitters across the frozen surface of the ocean to either side in a hundred broken fragments. The rumbling that accompanies this shattering of solid ice is like the low-throttled voice of the outboard engines. Three or four hundred yards of this and we stop. The pack ice is within twenty feet of the beach. We cannot go any farther. That we are only a hundred feet from our destination seems a part of the day, divinely fortuitous.

We climb up the bluff. Arctic-fox tracks in the patchy snow are fresh. Here and there on the tundra are bird feathers, remnants of the summer molt of hundreds of thousands of birds that have come this far north to nest, whose feathers blow inland and out to sea for weeks. Although we see no animals but a flock of snow geese in the distance, evidence of their residence and passage is everywhere. Within a few hundred feet I find caribou droppings. On a mossy tundra mound, like one a jaeger might use, I find two small bones that I know to be a ptarmigan's.

WE EXAMINE the upright, weathered logs and decide on the basis of these and several pieces of carved wood that this is, indeed, the border. No one, we reason, would erect something like this on a coast so unfrequented by humans if it were not. (This coast is ice-free only eight or ten weeks in the year.) Yet we are not sure. The bluff has a certain natural prominence, though the marker's placement seems arbitrary. But the romance of it—this foot in Canada, that one in Alaska—is fetching. The delightful weather and the presence of undisturbed animals has made us almost euphoric. It is, after days of bottom trawls in thirty-one-degree water, of cold hours of patient searching for seals, so clearly a holiday for us.

I will fly over this same spot a week later, under a

heavy overcast, forced down to two hundred feet above the water in a search for migrating bowhead whales. That trip, from the small settlement of Inuvik on the East Channel of the Mackenzie River in the Northwest Territories to Deadhorse, Alaska, will make this border both more real and more peculiar than it now appears. We will delay our arrival by circling over Inuvik until a Canadian customs officer can get there from the village of Tuktoyaktuk on the coast, though all we intend to do is to drop off an American scientist and buy gas. On our return trip we are required by law to land at the tiny village of Kaktovik to check through U.S. Customs. The entry through Kaktovik is so tenuous as to not exist at all. One might land, walk the mile to town, and find or not find the customs officer around. Should he not be there, the law requires we fly 250 miles south to Fort Yukon. If no one is there we are to fly on to Fairbanks before returning to Deadhorse on the coast, in order to reenter the country legally. These distances are immense. We could hardly carry the fuel for such a trip. And to fly inland would mean not flying the coast to look for whales, the very purpose of being airborne. We fly straight to Deadhorse, looking for whales. When we land we fill out forms to explain our actions and file them with the government.

Here, standing on the ground, the border seems nearly whimsical. The view over tens of square miles of white, frozen ocean and a vast expanse of tundra which rolls to the foot of snow-covered mountains is unimpeded. Such open space, on such a calm and innocent day as this, gives extraordinary release to the imagination. At such a remove—from horrible images of human death on borders ten thousand miles away, from the press of human anxiety one feels in a crowded city—at such a remove one is lulled nearly to foundering by the simple peace engendered, even at the border between two nations, by a single day of good weather.

As we turn to leave the monument, we see two swans coming toward us. They are immature tundra swans, in steel-gray plumage. Something odd is in their shape. Primary feathers. They have no primary feathers yet. Too young. And their parents, who should be with them, are nowhere to be seen. They are coming from the east, from Canada, paddling in a strip of water a few inches deep right at the edge of the beach. They show no fear of us, although they slow and are cautious. They extend their necks and open their pink bills to make gentle, rattling sounds. As they near the boat they stand up in the water and step ashore. They walk past us and on up the beach. Against the gritty coarseness of beach sand and the tundra-stained ice, their smooth gray feathers and the deep lucidity of their eyes vibrate with beauty. I watch them until they disappear from view. The chance they will be alive in two weeks is very slim. Perhaps it doesn't exist at all.

In two weeks I am thousands of miles south. In among the letters and magazines in six weeks of mail sitting on the table is a thick voter-registration pamphlet. One afternoon I sit down and read it. I try to read it with the conscientiousness of one who wishes to vote wisely. I think of Carl Sauer, whose ideas I admire. And of Wendell Berry, whose integrity and sense of land come to mind when I ponder any vote and the effect it might have. I think of the invisible borders of rural landscapes, of Frost pondering the value of fences. I read in the pamphlet of referendums on statewide zoning and of the annexation of rural lands, on which I am expected to vote. I read of federal legislative reapportionment and the realignment of my county's border with that of an Indian reservation, though these will not require my vote. I must review, again, how the districts of my state representative and state senator overlap and determine if I am included now within the bounds of a newly created county commissioner's territory.

These lines blur and I feel a choking coming up in my neck and my face flushing. I set the pamphlet on the arm of the chair and get up and walk outside. It is going to take weeks, again, to get home.

# The Bull Rider

WHAT ARE THESE, medieval eyes? Up close, under inch-long lashes, they bulge, hair-triggered, the size of cue balls.

Is this what alfalfa has wrought? 1428 lbs. 1701 lbs.

Bulls. A cleated hoof hits the door of a chute with a crack, with the speed of a middleweight's jab. The eyes roll. The head comes up and the wide, wet nose pries between two-by-eight boards. The chute door whines under his lean.

Bulls.

Shit.

*The Cowboy* This bull here's a little slow, but he's big, got lots of power, makes him fairly hard to ride. This one I went eighty points on about three years ago. Called him Joe Bananas. When I had him he was really good; he kicked good, he'd come around to the left. Big strong bull. Won Kennewick on him. This one here, he jumps and kicks, kinda walks on his toes. He's just really hard to ride. This one has a tendency to have a lot of downdraft. Every round he makes he pulls you down a little more in the hole. That Brahngus over there is strong all the time; reverses, comes back to the right, comes back to the left, jumps underneath himself, makes you want to jab out over his head. He'll make you bow down like that, then come up and smack your face with his head. Call it Frenching. Broke a jaw like that two years ago.

*The Contractor* In the old days, in my opinion, there were tough bull riders, but not as many of them. Today you have sixty bull riders at a rodeo, forty of them are liable to ride anything you got. You don't see it very often, but I know sooner or later even a bull that's never been ridden, thrown hundreds of guys, is gonna get rid. It's just like anything else. There's only so long they're gonna go before cowboys figure out a way to ride 'em.

You know, cowboys tell you the stock isn't as rank as it was in the old days, you don't see as many double-rank animals, and I don't believe that. What is it they say, "Feed the cowboy on road maps and diesel smoke for a while and see how he holds up"? We have more rodeos to go to now than we used to, we have less time between rodeos and more top quality bull riders and it all takes it out of the stock. The hauling is the hardest thing on 'em.

I could maybe breed bulls and come up with more mean ones, but that takes cows and a breeding operation and I just haven't got the time. I go down to Texas or Florida and try and buy a bull with a proven reputation. This year I've spent $10,000 for maybe fifteen head and only gotten two that I'm really satisfied with. Last year I paid $2,500 for a bull down in Texas that had never been ridden. Well, they had an amateur rider on him, he was in a small arena, they had about three clowns out there and two barrels and he was fresh and he was wild, I mean he put on a hell of a show. But he hasn't done a damn thing for me.

You have to look for something crossbred, something that's been out in the swamps down there and people only see once a year when they go to round 'em up. I like to have a little Mexican fighting bull in 'em too, so they hook and go for the clowns. Something like a purebred Brahma isn't worth a shit. They don't have a heart as big as this match. They won't buck, they lay down in the chutes, don't want to do nothing. You've got to get a Charolais or Brahngus, maybe a quarter Brahma, a little Brown Swiss. You want a bull with some heart.

If I have a young bull that's bucking for me, I like to keep him out awhile, put a lot of small, inexperienced riders up on him and let him throw 'em off. The more he throws off the more heart he gets, until he's so full of heart no one can ride him. Then one day he gets ridden and watch out; he'll go back in the pen and he'll try to tear the goddamn thing down. You just have to leave him alone for a few days while he works it out. It makes him madder than hell to get ridden. The best ones are the ones that are born with that feeling, but it's a hard thing to see when you go to buy one and damn near impossible to breed.

I try to take 'em off their feed and water early in the morning if it's an afternoon ride, so they get hungry, kinda gant and drawed down a little bit. Then I like to watch a bull rider take his shot. I don't think it's easier to ride bulls than any other event, but kids get the impression it's easier to learn because all you have is a bullrope and a pair of spurs and all you have to do is hold on for eight seconds, but a lot of them find out different.

*The Cowboy* I like to think about my bulls a day ahead of time, up to eight hours before a rodeo. I like to think really heavy on them, try to concentrate as much as I can on that bull if I know him. If I don't know him, just going through riding bulls in general in my mind. Then I like to forget about it while I'm at the rodeo until a half hour or hour before the bull ride and get myself pumped up, what we call it you know, get ourselves right, get the right kind of feeling.

*The Comer* The really rank bulls will turn over hard and you gotta blow over in there, get down in there away from that centrifugal force. His power will throw you to the outside again and you have to fight to get back in there. A really tricky bull will change direction so fast when he's spinning he'll leave you standing on the ground. When they get old, they get smart. A young bull will go on out there and buck his butt off. An old bull, he'll go two rounds in a spin and if he's not loosening you up, he's gonna go the other way. A real smart, rank bull will go three ways, try some trash, lay on his side.

With real rank bulls you don't plan nothing. You don't think "He's gonna go three jumps and then come back left" and just idle out of there ready for it. He might go one jump and then turn back and gas it, spin. That spinning, if you're not into it—there's one spot, you get out of it and you just have to keep trying to get back to it. Sometimes you get in there too far and you have to let yourself out; or you get out too far and you have to blow back in there. The whole ride you're thinking, "Jeeze, I'm in there too far," and you'll come out. Then you'll think, "Shit, I'm too far out," and you'll blow over in there. It's just in and out, in and out, and then the whistle goes and it just brings you out of a trance.

A bull, he'll be smooth and all of a sudden he'll be turkey, but a bronc, he'll jump and kick and he'll jerk you, jerk you till you get throwed off, just get worse and worse. Bull, he'll be smooth. If you're tight with him, he'll be smooth and then all of a sudden he'll just get you. You just gotta estimate the right place to be. If you're in the wrong place, he'll throw you off. If he jerks you, it's too late.

On a bronc you don't have to pump up until that first jump. You start your horse out and he'll jerk you and that'll get the adrenaline going you know and you spur—he'll blow you out the front end and you just set your feet, get your pump going. But bulls, if they jerk you like that the first jump they're gonna throw you off right there. That's the difference. That's why bull riders have to get so much more psyched up. None of this right-there-at-the-first-jump stuff.

*The Cowboy* I think maybe the difference between like a professional football player and cowboys is I love what I'm doing. There's not much money in it, but I love rodeo and I love riding bulls. So if I can win a thousand dollars here and two hundred over there, I feel good about it. Where I think the professional athlete in football, they do it for the money. Maybe there's a lot of pleasure in it but I think they do it for the money and I do it because I enjoy it.

*The Champ* You've gotta have try. If you don't have the try, you can have all the ability in the world and it's not going to work. And you have to learn to react without thinking. You don't have time to stop and think. If he moves hard to the right, *bang,* you gotta be there. All this has to come from being programmed beforehand. You've got on so many bulls, you've studied them over and over in your mind and it's programmed. If the bull kicks really good, you know you have to sit back on him a little bit; if he comes up in the front end, you know you have to get out over him. But you can't say, "Well, he's coming up in the front end, I gotta get over him," or "He's kicking, I gotta get back," or "He's turning back to the right or left, I gotta get in there"—you don't have time to think about it.

I use mental pictures before I ride; I just sit and try to visualize myself riding the bull, over and over and over, and doing it—everything he does. If he moves to the right, I picture myself making that same move with him, being in the same timing with him. It's funny: When I'm really riding good, when I'm pulling my rope in that chute, there's no doubt in my mind: I know I am the master.

I'll tell you what: I started out with nothing. Me and my wife got married and lived in a rented trailer house. I set a goal that I had to have a place to live of my own. The next year we bought a nice trailer home. I set the goal that I had to have the trailer home when I wasn't winning anything at all. The deal came up for it and I went down to Phoenix and won bull riding. It was like I was due.

There's up and down in rodeo, there's that element of being cold and being hot, riding good, drawing good. You go through a cold streak and it's so easy to get down on yourself, and your riding starts to deteriorate. Good little bulls are bucking you off. I think this is where the tough of the tough bull riders come through. They don't get down on themselves when they get in a cold streak; when a good bull does come along they're right there, and they win. They're ready. I think that's the biggest thing about winning. There are so many people who hope to win; the winners are the ones who expect to win. It's your mental attitude, having your head right, that's the most important thing. It's a private thing, and it's a hard medium to hit, you know. You're affected by other people's attitudes. You can be around a loser and never know it.

When I started, my ultimate goal was to win the World's. When I finally won it, I hadn't thought about winning it three times, just once. I didn't have the desire to win it again and it left me with a kind of what-do-you-do-now attitude. I was the best there was in the field. The only thing I could do was be the best again or settle down and try something else. So I settled down to buying a ranch and getting some other things going. I like to keep my status up, but I know I'll never win the World's again. I pushed it five years and worked a hundred to a hundred and forty rodeos a year. I've got my wife and a beautiful little boy and I want to be home with them.

*The Cowboy* I'll tell you what: if we didn't have them clowns we couldn't ride bulls.

*The Clown* I think a bull rider exemplifies in this day and age the spirit of the West more than anything else Western. He is the ultimate. The man goes into the business knowing there's danger involved. It's not the danger of just being stepped on, or riding a bull—having trouble getting something rode—it's a matter of getting away from a bull that he knows is out to hurt him when he gets off. The man hired out to be tough, he's gonna be tough when he gets in there, and as far as I'm concerned there's a lot of people that don't ride bulls that are every bit as tough; but these fellows, they've all proven themselves, the fact that they have that courage, that extra little bit of I-don't-give-a-hoot-what-happens, I'll-be-there.

The urge to win, the will to win, is such a wonderful thing and I can't say enough about it because it's probably what motivates the whole cussed thing. Just a guy wanting to do better. The fellow who wants to coast along and wait for tomorrow and see what it brings, that's what he'll do. And probably the rest of his life he'll do that, and he'll probably do fine, he'll never have any problems, but he won't ever do anything exceptional. To these fellows, the exceptional thing is being able to do something just a little above the horizon, something that other people can't ordinarily do.

I've always kind of operated on the principle that a man can do anything in the world he puts his mind to as long as he feels he can do it, deep down inside feels he can do it, he can handle it.

I haven't been a flashy bullfighter, a man with a lot of fancy moves, but I've prided myself on what I call an earned run average and in this business it's just as apropos as it is in baseball: the amount of guys you end up leaving on the ground to be drug off. I've got a pretty good one over the years and I'm proud of it. And to me, that means a lot. I've tried my best to make a bull show good for a man, tried my best to pull the bull off him when he was down, whether it was my boy or somebody else's.

In this business if you're not tough they're gonna find out damn quick. You can't bullshit with the bull. You've come to the facts. You are or you aren't; they separate them right quick. It's too bad in a way politicians can't get in on something like this. They'd learn about winners and losers. You can't stand out there and tell a funny story.

*The Comer* That bull there, Lucky Three of Flying 5, cost me the national finals last year. He threw me off at San Francisco. All I had to do was ride him and I woulda went to the finals. All I needed to win was $120. And he threw me off, the sonofabitch. I tried like a bitch. You know, you hit the ground—ktschsch—and NATIONAL FINALS GONE DOWN THE DRAIN! This whole year is washed up! You drive down the road, start at Portland, the first rodeo of the year, and you're in the lead for the next year.

You know sometimes you get down, you start entering all these rodeos, you get, *thump, thump,* thrown off, and you go to thinking the only way you can keep from getting throwed off two a week is by entering one. There's no way around it. You just get down.

*The Cowboy* The fans, I think they come for the thrill. They like to see people get hurt, they come to see that.

*The Wreck* I'm probably one of the few men that's been crippled so many times I can't win very much. I broke a lot of bones in me.

How many?

Thirty.

Really? What are you nursing now?

My brother and I were figuring it out—Nothing. I'm in top condition except for this damn sore leg he tramped on today.

What about your knee, is that just a protection, that steel brace?

Great big bull stepped on me one time . . . stretched those two big heavy tendons back here. If I don't wear metal support to keep the leg from twisting at the knee, those two tendons get sore and I can't lift on the foot.

What was that thing you had on your chest?

That's a shoulder harness, to keep my arms from overreaching. You can touch your ear like this easy, but if you come around with your arm like this—there's a disc in your spine that can slide out. It controls two leaders in your shoulder. If you come over like this, these two leaders will cross, and they don't come back by themselves. You got to get a chiropractor to put them back in. It hurts so damn much you can't lift your arm out.

Why do you still ride bulls if you've been hurt so many times? I mean didn't they pronounce you dead after a ride in the arena in Calgary last year?

When I'm 35 or 40 I'll lose my ability and I won't be able to, even if I want to.

How old are you now?

Thirty-one.

When did you start riding bulls?

When I was eighteen.

Have you ever done really well?

Oh, I had about a $5500 year about eight years ago. The following year I broke my head. It damn near killed me.

I still don't understand why if you've been wrecked so many times, thirty broken bones, and you can make ten times as much running a derrick why you don't run your derrick. Why keep riding bulls?

I'm going to answer that in a darn crude way. Is this a live interview?

No, it's just for my—

The working world is so full of boot-licking, ass-wiping individuals that you can only stand it for about ten or twelve months at a time.

And that's why you keep coming back to ride bulls?

Here I'm my own boss.

Why do those people turn your stomach?

I don't like to see a man that's buttered up the boss get ahead of a man that's worked for it but won't do that sort of thing.

Do you think that's what makes cowboys different?

In my point of view, most cowboys, with time, damn sure learn humility. That's kind of a strong word but I looked it up in the dictionary one day and that's what I mean.

*The Cowboy* Some day you're gonna get throwed off and you're not gonna know why. But if you go home and think about it for about two or three hours, it'll come to you, the exact thing that threw you off.

You know, the thing is not to be the champ, it's to be a better cowboy. And you've got to crave it, you've got to crave getting on those bulls to be any good. When you quit craving it you get hurt.

*The Comer* In this sport there's no coaches to pump you up, no trainers, no travel allowance, no whirlpools to put you in, no nothing, just yourself. I used to wrestle in high school: to win you had to be cold with anticipation, hungry.

On occasion some of the guys use the bottle, just go out and get wiped out. But cowboys don't drink every night, they go out one night and get dead level and they don't drink for a month. That's the way I do it. I'll just get right out of it. Course I'd like to be twenty-one so I could go into a bar legal and hustle some women. Some guys drink, some guys hustle women, they all have their pastimes. Cowboys, you know, spend a lot of time alone. You *know* some of these women are saying, "I'd just like to fucking fall in love with that guy," it's just natural. I don't like going out with a bunch of speed freak models, I don't like drugs. Not natural. Sex I like. Natural sex, the Cadillac of simple pleasures.

I'll tell you what on dope: cowboys, they'll try it, but it's just not tradition. Most cowboys got a lot of tradition in them, otherwise they wouldn't be rodeoing. Fathers kind of brought them into it. Lot of them been to college and you can't hardly get through college without catching the clap and smoking some pot anymore. But they don't stick to it. They all try it, but they don't pack it with them. I'd rather get high on good music. Sex and good music. Booze really isn't any good either.

*The Cowboy* I got three years of school in, then I quit, wanted to rodeo too much. I want to rodeo at least another five or six years. I have goals set for myself. If I can achieve these goals in less time than that I might quit then.

To me rodeo is a lot of fun and I like doing it, but I can't see no future in it. There's not enough money where a guy can make a decent living. A guy has to have his money invested in something solid. I'd like to get into my own business. My dad, he raises a lot of cattle and we're kinda in partnership. I'd like to get a place of my own in a few years and run some cows.

*The Comer* This here rodeo is just making a mockery out of the cowboy. Cowboy, you know, he doesn't take that much concern, but the reason he's getting a little irate now is expenses are getting so high. Inflation. Christ, this prize money at this rodeo and rodeos all over the U.S. hasn't gone up five percent in the last hundred years hardly, and that ain't even bank interest rates anymore, five percent. Cowboys are getting a little uptight because they don't want to quit rodeoing you know.

People get down on cowboys. Guy'll go into a restaurant and he'll eat and he'll just pay for his meal and go. And you know he's paying these jacked-up prices in every rodeo town he goes to. Well, the waitress, she'll get peeved because he didn't leave a big tip. Well, Christ, the poor cowboy he can't even afford it. And yet people think, "Oh, hell, he's professional, big cowboy you know. He's rich." This year, unless you're running constantly, you can just barely get by. And this rodeo's addicting you know. You can't just get out of it. It gets in your veins.

Hell, cowboy, he's just trying to make it down the road.

*Hey Brian, what're you up on?*

*Rattler.*

*Christensen Brothers bull?*

*Yeah, he ain't worth a shit. I'm gonna go with him for three or four seconds and if he ain't doing nothing spur him, ride him like a bareback horse.*

*He's maybe fifty-seven, fifty-eight points.*

*If I fall off it don't matter anyway. If I spur the shit out of him I might get a sixty-four. Sixty-four might go in the last hole in the finals. Then I might draw a rank sonofabitch and if I ride him then I can win first.*

He does.

Young boys in the grandstands hurl water balloons that burst across the shoulders of bulls in the pens below.

# A Presentation of Whales

ON THAT SECTION of the central Oregon coast on the evening of June 16, 1979, gentle winds were blowing onshore from the southwest. It was fifty-eight degrees. Under partly cloudy skies the sea was running with four-foot swells at eight-second intervals. Moderately rough. State police cadets Jim Clark and Steve Bennett stood at the precipitous edge of a foredune a few miles south of the town of Florence, peering skeptically into the dimness over a flat, gently sloping beach. Near the water's edge they could make out a line of dark shapes, and what they had taken for a practical joke, the exaggeration a few moments before of a man and a woman in a brown Dodge van with a broken headlight, now sank in for the truth.

Clark made a hasty, inaccurate count and plunged with Bennett down the back of the dune to their four-wheel-drive. Minutes before, they had heard the voice of Corporal Terry Crawford over the radio; they knew he was patrolling in Florence. Rather than call him, they drove the six miles into town and parked across the street from where he was issuing a citation to someone for excessive noise. When Crawford had finished, Clark went over and told him what they had seen. Crawford drove straight to the Florence State Police office and phoned his superiors in Newport, forty-eight miles up the coast. At that point the news went out over police radios: thirty-six large whales, stranded and apparently still alive, were on the beach a mile south of the mouth of the Siuslaw River.

There were, in fact, forty-one whales—twenty-eight females and thirteen males, at least one of them dying or already dead. There had never been a stranding quite like it. It was first assumed that they were gray whales, common along the coast, but they were sperm whales: *Physeter catodon*. Deep-ocean dwellers. They ranged in age from ten to fifty-six and in length from thirty to thirty-eight feet. They were apparently headed north when they beached around 7:30 P.M. on an ebbing high tide.

The information shot inland by phone, crossing the Coast Range to radio and television stations in the more-populous interior of Oregon, in a highly charged form: giant whales stranded on a public beach accessible by paved road on a Saturday night, still alive. Radio announcers urged listeners to head for the coast to "save the whales." In Eugene and Portland, Greenpeace volunteers, already alerted by the police, were busy throwing sheets and blankets into their cars. They would soak them in the ocean, to cool the whales.

The news moved as quickly through private homes and taverns on the central Oregon coast, passed by people monitoring the police bands. In addition to phoning Greenpeace—an international organization with a special interest in protecting marine mammals—the police contacted the Oregon State University Marine Science Center in South Beach near Newport, and the Oregon Institute of Marine Biology in Charleston, fifty-eight miles south of Florence. Bruce Mate, a marine mammalogist at the OSU Center, phoned members of the Northwest Regional [Stranding] Alert Network and people in Washington, D.C.

By midnight, the curious and the awed were crowded on the beach, cutting the night with flashlights. Drunks, ignoring the whales' sudden thrashing, were trying to walk up and down on their backs. A collie barked incessantly; flash cubes burst at the huge, dark forms. Two men inquired about reserving some of the teeth, for scrimshaw. A federal agent asked police to move people back, and the first mention of disease was in the air. Scientists arrived with specimen bags and rubber gloves and fishing knives. Greenpeace members, one dressed in a bright orange flight suit, came with a large banner. A man burdened with a television camera labored over the foredune after them. They wished to tie a rope to one whale's flukes, to drag it back into the ocean. The police began to congregate with the scientists, looking for a rationale to control the incident.

In the intensifying confusion, as troopers motioned onlookers back (to "restrain the common herd of unqualified mankind," wrote one man later in an angry letter-to-the-editor), the thinking was that, somehow, the whales might be saved. Neal Langbehn, a federal protection officer with the National Marine Fisheries Service, denied permission to one scientist to begin removing teeth and taking blood samples. In his report later he would write: "It was my feeling that the whales should be given their best chance to survive."

This hope was soon deemed futile, as it had appeared to most of the scientists from the beginning—the animals were hemorrhaging under the crushing weight of their own flesh and were beginning to suffer irreversible damage from heat exhaustion. The scientific task became one of securing as much data as possible.

As dawn bloomed along the eastern sky, people who had driven recreational vehicles illegally over the dunes and onto the beach were issued citations and turned back. Troopers continued to warn people over bullhorns to please stand away from the whales. The Oregon Parks Department, whose responsibility the beach was, wanted no part of the growing confusion. The U.S. Forest Service, with jurisdiction over land in the Oregon Dunes National Recreation Area down to the foredune, was willing to help, but among all the agencies there was concern over limited budgets; there were questions, gently essayed, about the conflict of state and federal enforcement powers over the body parts of an endangered species. A belligerent few in the crowd shouted objections as the first syringes appeared, and yelled to scientists to produce permits that allowed them to interfere in the death of an endangered species.

Amid this chaos, the whales, sealed in their slick black neoprene skins, mewed and clicked. They slammed glistening flukes on the beach, jarring the muscles of human thighs like Jell-O at a distance of a hundred yards. They rolled their dark, purple-brown eyes at the scene and blinked.

They lay on the western shore of North America like forty-one derailed boxcars at dawn on a Sunday morning, and in the days that followed, the worst and the best of human behavior was shown among them.

THE SPERM WHALE, for many, is the most awesome creature of the open seas. Imagine a forty-five-year-old male fifty feet long, a slim, shiny black animal with a white jaw and marbled belly cutting the surface of green ocean water at twenty knots. Its flat forehead protects a sealed chamber of exceedingly fine oil; sunlight sparkles in rivulets running off folds in its corrugated back. At fifty tons it is the largest carnivore on earth. Its massive head, a third of its body length, is scarred with the beak, sucker, and claw marks of giant squid, snatched out of subterranean canyons a mile below, in a region without light, and brought writhing to the surface. Imagine a four-hundred-pound heart the size of a chest of drawers driving five gallons of blood at a stroke through its aorta: a meal of forty salmon moving slowly down twelve-hundred feet of intestine; the blinding, acrid fragrance of a two-hundred-pound wad of gray ambergris lodged somewhere along the way; producing sounds more shrill than we can hear—like children shouting on a distant playground—and able to sort a cacophony of noise: electric crackling of shrimp, groaning of undersea quakes, roar of upwellings, whining of porpoise, hum of oceanic cables. With skin as sensitive as the inside of your wrist.

What makes them awesome is not so much these things, which are discoverable, but the mysteries that shroud them. They live at a remarkable distance from us and we have no *Pioneer II* to penetrate their world. Virtually all we know of sperm whales we have learned on the slaughter decks of oceangoing whalers and on the ways at shore stations. We do not even know how many there are; in December 1978, the Scientific Committee of the International Whaling Commission said it could not set a quota for a worldwide sperm whale kill—so little was known that any number written down would be ridiculous.*

*A quota of 5000 was nevertheless set. In June 1979, within days of the Florence stranding but apparently unrelated to it, the IWC dropped the 1980 world sperm whale quota to 2203 and set aside the Indian Ocean as a sanctuary. (By 1987 the quota was 0, though special exemptions permit some 200 sperm whales still to be taken worldwide.)

The sperm whale, in all its range of behaviors—from the enraged white bull called Mocha Dick that stove whaling ships off the coast of Peru in 1810, to a nameless female giving birth to a fourteen-foot, one-ton calf in equatorial waters in the Pacific—remains distant. The general mystery is enhanced by specific mysteries: the sperm whale's brain is larger than the brain of any other creature that ever lived. Beyond the storage of incomprehensible amounts of information, we do not know what purpose such size serves. And we do not know what to make of its most distinctive anatomical feature, the spermaceti organ. An article in *Scientific American,* published several months before the stranding, suggests that the whale can control the density of its spermaceti oil, thereby altering its specific gravity to assist it in diving. It is argued also that the huge organ, located in the head, serves as a means of generating and focusing sound, but there is not yet any agreement on these speculations.

Of the many sperm whale strandings in recorded history, only three have been larger than the one in Oregon. The most recent was of fifty-six on the eastern Baja coast near Playa San Rafael on January 6, 1979. But the Florence stranding is perhaps the most remarkable. Trained scientists arrived almost immediately; the site was easily accessible, with even an airstrip close by. It was within an hour's drive of two major West Coast marine-science centers. And the stranding seemed to be of a whole social unit. That the animals were still alive meant live blood specimens could be taken. And by an uncanny coincidence, a convention of the American Society of Mammalogists was scheduled to convene June 18 at Oregon State University in Corvallis, less than a two-hour drive away. Marine experts from all over the country would be there. (As it turned out, some of them would not bother to come over; others would secure access to the beach only to take photographs; still others would show up in sports clothes—all they had—and plunge into the gore that by the afternoon of June 18 littered the beach.)

The state police calls to Greenpeace on the night of June 16 were attempts to reach informed people to direct a rescue. Michael Piper of Greenpeace, in Eugene, was the first to arrive with a small group at about 1:30 A.M., just after a low tide at 12:59 A.M.

I RAN RIGHT OUT of my shoes," Piper says. The thought that they would still be alive—clicking and murmuring, their eyes tracking human movement, lifting their flukes, whooshing warm air from their blowholes—had not penetrated. But as he ran into the surf to fill a bucket to splash water over their heads, the proportions of the stranding and the impending tragedy overwhelmed him.

"I knew, almost from the beginning, that we were not going to get them out of there, and that even if we did, their chances of survival were a million to one," Piper said.

Just before dawn, a second contingent of Greenpeace

volunteers arrived from Portland. A Canadian, Michael Bailey, took charge and announced there was a chance with the incoming tide that one of the smaller animals could be floated off the beach and towed to sea (weights ranged from an estimated three and a half to twenty-five tons). Bruce Mate, who would become both scientific and press coordinator on the beach (the latter to his regret), phoned the Port of Coos Bay to see if an ocean-going tug or fishing vessel would be available to anchor offshore and help—Bailey's crew would ferry lines through the surf with a Zodiac boat. No one in Coos Bay was interested. A commercial helicopter service with a Skycrane capable of lifting nine tons also begged off. A call to the Coast Guard produced a helicopter, but people there pronounced any attempt to sky-tow a whale too dangerous.

The refusal of help combined with the apparent futility of the effort precipitated a genuinely compassionate gesture: Bailey strode resolutely into the freezing water and, with twenty-five or thirty others, amid flailing flukes, got a rope around the tail of an animal that weighed perhaps three or four tons. The waves knocked them down and the whale yanked them over, but they came up sputtering, to pull again. With the buoyancy provided by the incoming tide they moved the animal about thirty feet. The effort was heroic and ludicrous. As the rope began to cut into the whale's flesh, as television cameramen and press photographers crowded in, Michael Piper gave up his place on the rope in frustration and waded ashore. Later he would remark that, for some, the whale was only the means to a political end—a dramatization of the plight of whales as a species. The distinction between the suffering individual, its internal organs hemorrhaging, its flukes sliced by the rope, and the larger issue, to save the species, confounded Piper.

A photograph of the Greenpeace volunteers pulling the whale showed up nationally in newspapers the next day. A week later, a marine mammalogist wondered if any more damaging picture could have been circulated. It would convince people something could have been done, when in fact, he said, the whales were doomed as soon as they came ashore.

For many, transfixed on the beach by their own helplessness, the value of the gesture transcended the fact.

By midmorning Piper was so disturbed, so embarrassed by the drunks and by people wrangling to get up on the whales or in front of photographers, that he left. As he drove off through the crowds (arriving now by the hundreds, many in campers and motor homes), gray whales were seen offshore, with several circling sperm whales. "The best thing we could have done," Piper said, alluding to this, "was offer our presence, to be with them while they were alive, to show some compassion."

Irritated by a callous (to him) press that seemed to have only one question—Why did they come ashore? —Piper had blurted out that the whales may have come ashore "because they were tired of running" from commercial whalers. Scientists scoffed at the remark, but

Piper, recalling it a week later, would not take it back. He said it was as logical as any other explanation offered in those first few hours.

Uneasy philosophical disagreement divided people on the beach from the beginning. Those for whom the stranding was a numinous event were estranged by the clowning of those who regarded it as principally entertainment. A few scientists irritated everyone with their preemptive, self-important air. When they put chain saws to the lower jaws of dead sperm whales lying only a few feet from whales not yet dead, there were angry shouts of condemnation. When townspeople kept at bay—"This is history, dammit," one man screamed at a state trooper, "and I want my kids to see it!"—saw twenty reporters, each claiming an affiliation with the same weekly newspaper, gain the closeness to the whales denied them, there were shouts of cynical derision.

"The effect of all this," said Michael Gannon, director of a national group called Oregonians Cooperating to Protect Whales, of the undercurrent of elitism and outrage, "was that it interfered with the spiritual and emotional ability of people to deal with the phenomenon. It was like being at a funeral where you were not allowed to mourn."

BOB WARREN, a patrolman with the U.S. Forest Service, said he was nearly brought to tears by what faced him Sunday morning. "I had no conception of what a whale beaching would be like. I was apprehensive about it, about all the tourists and the law-enforcement atmosphere. When I drove up, the whole thing hit me in the stomach: I saw these *numbers,* these damn orange numbers—41, 40, 39—spray-painted on these dying animals. The media were coming on like the marines, in taxicabs, helicopters, low-flying aircraft. Biologists were saying, 'We've got to *euthanize* them.' It made me sick."

By this time Sunday morning, perhaps five hundred people had gathered; the crowd would swell to more than two thousand before evening, in spite of a drizzling rain. The state trooper who briefed Warren outlined the major problems: traffic was backing up on the South Jetty Road almost five miles to U.S. 101; the whales' teeth were "as valuable as gold" and individuals with hammers and saws had been warned away already; people were sticking their hands in the whales' mouths and were in danger of being killed by the pounding flukes; and there was a public-health problem—the whales might have come ashore with a communicable disease. (According to several experts, the danger to public health was minor, but in the early confusion it served as an excuse to keep the crowd back so scientists could work. Ironically, the threat would assume a life of its own two days later and scientists would find themselves working frantically ahead of single-minded state burial crews.)

One of the first things Warren and others did was to rope off the whales with orange ribbon and lath stakes, establishing a line beyond which the public was no longer permitted. Someone thoughtful among them ran the ribbon close enough to one whale to allow people to peer into the dark eyes, to see scars left by struggling squid, lamprey eels, and sharp boulders on the ocean floor, the patches of diatoms growing on the skin, the marbling streaking back symmetrically from the genital slit, the startlingly gentle white mouth ("What a really beautiful and chaste-looking mouth!" Melville wrote. "From floor to ceiling lined, or rather papered with a glistening white membrane, glossy as bridal satins"), to see the teeth, gleaming in the long, almost absurdly narrow jaw. In *The Year of the Whale,* Victor Scheffer describes the tooth as "creamy white, a cylinder lightly curved, a thing of art which fits delightfully in the palm of my hand."

The temptation to possess—a Polaroid of oneself standing over a whale, a plug of flesh removed with a penknife, a souvenir squid beak plucked deftly from an exposed intestine by a scientist—was almost palpable in the air.

"From the beginning," Warren continued, "I was operating on two levels: as a law-enforcement officer with a job, and as a person." He escorted people away from the whales, explaining as well as he could the threat of disease, wishing himself to reach out with them, to touch the animals. He recalls his rage watching people poke at a sensitive area under the whales' eyes to make them react, and calmly directing people to step back, to let the animals die in peace. Nothing could be done, he would say. How do you know? they would ask. He didn't.

Warren was awed by the sudden, whooshing breath that broke the silence around an animal perhaps once every fifteen minutes, and saddened by the pitiable way some of them were mired with their asymmetrical blowhole sanded in, dead. Near those still breathing he drove in lath stakes with the word LIVE written on them. The hopelessness of it, he said, and the rarity of the event were rendered absurd by his having to yell into a bullhorn, by the blood on the beach, the whales' blinking, the taunters hoisting beer cans to the police.

One of the things about being human, Warren reflected, is learning to see beyond the vulgar. Along with the jocose in the crowd, he said, there were hundreds who whispered to each other, as if in a grove of enormous trees. And faces that looked as though they were awaiting word of relatives presumed dead in an air crash. He remembers in particular a man in his forties, "dressed in polyesters," who stood with his daughter in a tidal pool inside the barrier, splashing cool water on a whale. Warren asked them to please step back. "Why?" the man asked. Someone in the crowd yelled an obscenity at Warren. Warren thought to himself: Why is there no room for the decency of this gesture?

THE LEAST UNDERSTOOD and perhaps most disruptive incident on the beach on that first day was the attempt of veterinarians to kill the whales, first by injecting M–99, a morphine-base drug, then by ramming pipes into their pleural cavities to collapse their lungs, and finally by severing major arteries and letting them bleed to death. The techniques were crude, but no one knew enough sperm whale anatomy or physiology to make a clean job of it, and no one wanted to try some of the alternatives—from curare to dynamite—that would have made the job quicker. The ineptitude of the veterinarians caused them a private embarrassment to which they gave little public expression. Their frustration at their own inability to do anything to "help" the whales was exacerbated by nonscientists demanding from the sidelines that the animals be "put out of their misery." (The reasons for attempting euthanasia were poorly understood, philosophically and medically, and the issue nagged people long after the beach bore not a trace of the incident itself.)

As events unfolded on the beach, the first whale died shortly after the stranding, the last almost thirty-six hours later; suffocation and overheating were the primary causes. By waiting as long as they did to try to kill some of the animals and by allowing others to die in their own time, pathologists, toxicologists, parasitologists, geneticists, and others got tissues of poor quality to work with.* The disappointment was all the deeper because never had so many scientists been in a position

*A subsequent report, presented at a marine-mammals conference in Seattle in October 1979, made it clear that the whales began to suffer the effects of heat stress almost immediately. The breakdown of protein structures in their tissues made discovery of a cause of death difficult; from the beginning, edema, capillary dilation, and hemorrhaging made their recovery unlikely. Ice, seawater pumps, and tents for shade rather than Zodiac boats and towlines were suggested if useful tissue was to be salvaged in the future from large whales.

to gather so much information. (Even with this loss and an initial lack of suitable equipment—chemicals to preserve tissues, blood-analysis kits, bone saws, flensing knives—the small core of twenty or so scientists "increased human knowledge about sperm whales several hundred percent," according to Mate.)

The fact that almost anything learned was likely to be valuable was meager consolation to scientists hurt by charges that they were cold and brutal people, irreverently jerking fetuses from the dead. Among these scientists were people who sat alone in silence, who departed in anger, and who broke down and cried.

NO ONE KNOWS why whales strand. It is almost always toothed whales that do, rather than baleen whales, most commonly pilot whales, Atlantic white-sided dolphins, false killer whales, and sperm whales—none of which are ordinarily found close to shore. Frequently they strand on gently sloping beaches. Among the more tenable explanations: 1) extreme social cohesion, where one sick animal is relentlessly followed ashore by many healthy animals; 2) disease or parasitic infection that affects the animals' ability to navigate: 3) harassment, by predators and, deliberate or inadvertent, by humans; 4) a reversion to phylogentically primitive escape behavior—get out of the water—precipitated by stress.

At a public meeting in Florence—arranged by the local librarian to explain to a public kept off the beach what had happened, and to which invited scientists did not come—other explanations were offered. Someone had noticed whales splashing in apparent confusion near a river dredge and thought the sound of its engines might have driven the whales crazy. Local fishermen said there had been an unusual, near-shore warm current on June 16, with a concentration of plankton so thick they had trouble penetrating it with their depth finders. Another suggestion was that the whales might have been temporarily deranged by poisons in diatoms concentrated in fish they were eating.

The seventy-five or so people at the meeting seemed irritated that there was no answer, as did local reporters looking for an end to the story. Had scientists been there it is unlikely they could have suggested one. The beach was a gently sloping one, but the Florence whales showed no evidence of parasitism or disease, and modern research makes it clear that no single explanation will suffice. For those who would blame the machinations of modern man, scientists would have pointed out that strandings have been recorded since the time of Aristotle's *Historia animalium.*

The first marine biologist to arrive on the beach, at 3:30 A.M. Sunday, was Michael Graybill, a young instructor from the Oregon Institute of Marine Biology. He was not as perplexed as other scientists would be; a few months before he had dismantled the rotting carcass of a fifty-six-foot sperm whale that had washed ashore thirty miles south of Florence.

Graybill counted the animals, identified them as

sperm whales, noted that, oddly, there were no nursing calves or obviously young animals, and that they all seemed "undersized." He examined their skin and eyes, smelled their breath, looked for signs of oral and anal discharge, and began the task of sexing and measuring the animals.

Driving to the site, Graybill worried most about someone "bashing their teeth out" before he got there. He wasn't worried about communicable disease; he was "willing to gamble" on that. He regarded efforts to save the whales, however, as unnatural interference in their death. Later, he cynically observed "how much 'science' took place at the heads of sperm whales" where people were removing teeth; and he complained that if they really cared about the worldwide fate of whales, Greenpeace volunteers would have stayed to help scientists with postmortems. (Some did. Others left because they could not stand to watch the animals die.)

BEGINNING SUNDAY MORNING, scientists had their first chance to draw blood from live, unwounded sperm whales (they used comparatively tiny one-and-a-half-inch, 18-gauge hypodermic needles stuck in vessels near the surface of the skin on the flukes). With the help of a blue, organic tracer they estimated blood volume at five hundred gallons. In subsequent stages, blubber, eyes, teeth, testicles, ovaries, stomach contents, and specific tissues were removed—the teeth for aging, the eyes for corneal cells to discover genetic relationships within the group. Postmortems were performed on ten females; three near-term fetuses were removed. An attempt was made to photograph the animals systematically.

The atmosphere on the beach shifted perceptibly over the next six days. On Sunday, a cool, cloudy day during which it rained, as many as three thousand people may have been on the beach. Police finally closed the access road to the area to discourage more from coming. Attempts to euthanize the animals continued, the jaws of the dead were being sawed off, and, in the words of one observer, "there was a television crew with a backdrop of stranded whales every twenty feet on the foredune."

By Monday the crowds were larger, but, in the estimation of a Forest Service employee, "of a higher quality. The type of people who show up at an automobile accident were gone; these were people who really wanted to see the whales. It was a four-and-a-half-mile walk in from the highway, and I talked with a woman who was seven months pregnant who made it and a man in a business suit and dress shoes who drove all the way down from Seattle."

Monday afternoon the crowds thinned. The beach had become a scene of postmortem gore sufficient to turn most people away. The outgoing tide had carried off gallons of blood and offal, drawing spiny dogfish sharks and smoothhound sharks into the breakers. As the animals died, scientists cut into them to relieve gaseous pressure—the resultant explosions could be heard half a mile away. A forty-pound chunk of liver whizzed by someone's back-turned shoulders; sixty feet of pearly-gray intestine unfurled with a snap against the sky. By evening the beach was covered with more than a hundred tons of intestines. Having to open the abdominal cavities so precipitately precluded, to the scientists' dismay, any chance of an uncontaminated examination.

By Tuesday the beach was closed to the public. The whale carcasses were being prepared for burning and burial, a task that would take four days, and reporters had given up asking why the stranding had happened, to comment on the stench.

THE MAN RESPONSIBLE for coordinating scientific work at the stranding, thirty-three-year-old Bruce Mate, is well regarded by his colleagues. Deborah Duffield, a geneticist from Portland State University, reiterated the feelings of several when she said of him: "The most unusual thing was that he got all of us with our different, sometimes competing, interests to work together. You can't comprehend what an extraordinary achievement that is in a situation like this."

On the beach Mate was also the principal source of information for the press. Though he was courteous to interviewers and careful not to criticize a sometimes impatient approach, one suspected he was disturbed by the role and uncertain what, if anything, he owed the nonscientific community.

In his small, cramped office at the Marine Science Center in South Beach, Mate agreed that everyone involved—scientists, environmentalists, the police, the state agencies, the public—took views that were occasionally in opposition and that these views were often proprietary. He thought it was the business of science to obtain data and physical specimens on the beach, thereby acquiring rights of "ownership," and yet he acknowledged misgivings about this because he and others involved are to some extent publicly funded scientists.

The task that faced him was deceptively simple: get as much information as possible off the beach before the burning crews, nervous about a public-health hazard and eager to end the incident, destroyed the animals. But what about the way science dominated the scene, getting the police, for example, to keep the crowd away so science could exercise its proprietary interest? "I don't know how to cope with the public's desire to come and see. Letting those few people onto the beach would have precluded our getting that much more information to give to a much larger, national audience."

What about charges that science operated in a cold-blooded and, in the case of trying to collapse the whales' lungs, ignorant way? "Coming among these whales, watching them die and in some cases helping them to die—needless suffering is almost incomprehensible to me . . ." Mate paused, studied the papers on his desk, unsatisfied, it seemed, with his tack; ". . . there are moral and ethical questions here. It's like dealing with terminal cancer."

No one, he seemed to suggest, liked how fast it had all happened.

Had he been worried about anything on the beach? "Yes! I was appalled at the way professional people were going about {postmortems} without gloves. I was afraid for the Greenpeace people in a potentially life-threatening situation in the surf." He was also afraid that it would all get away from him because of the unknowns. What, in fact, *did* one save when faced with such an enormous amount of bone and tissue? But he came away happy. "This was the greatest scientific shot anyone ever had with large whales." After a moment he added, "If it happened tomorrow, we would be four times better."

Sitting at his desk, nursing a pinched nerve in his back, surrounded by phone messages from the press, he seemed seasoned.

MATE'S TWENTY-SEVEN-YEAR-OLD graduate assistant, Jim Harvey, arrived on the beach at dawn on Sunday. At the first sight of the whales from the top of the dunes, strung out nose to flukes in a line five or six hundred yards long, the waves of a high tide breaking over them, Harvey simply sat down, awestruck at their size and number. He felt deeply sad, too, but as he drew near he felt "a rush of exhilaration, because there was so much information to be gathered." He could not get over the feeling, as he worked, of the size of them. (One afternoon a scientist stood confounded in a whale's abdomen, asking a colleague next to him, "Where's the liver?")

Deborah Duffield said of her experience on the

beach: "It hurt me more than watching human beings die. I couldn't cope with the pain, the futility. . . . I just turned into myself. It brought out the scientist in me." Another scientist spoke of his hostility toward the sullen crowd, of directing that anger at himself, of becoming cold and going to work.

For Harvey and others, there was one incident that broke scientific concentration and brought with it a feeling of impropriety. Several scientists had started to strip blubber from a dead whale. Suddenly the whale next to it began pounding the beach with its flukes. The pounding continued for fifteen minutes—lifting and slamming the flukes to the left, lifting and slamming the flukes to the right.

When the animal quieted, they resumed work.

"Scientists rarely get a chance to express their feelings," Harvey said. "I was interested in other people's views, and I wanted to share mine, which are biological. I noticed some people who sat quietly for a long time behind the barriers in religious stances. I very much wanted to know their views. So many of the people who came down here were so sympathetic and full of concern—I wished I had the time to talk to them all." Harvey remembered something vividly. On the first day he put his face near the blowhole of one of the whales: a cylinder of clean, warm, humid air almost a foot in diameter blew back his hair.

* * *

"MY VIEW ON IT," said Joe Davis of the Oregon Parks Department, "wasn't the scientific part. My thought on it now is how nice it would have been to have been somewhere else." His smile falls between wryness and regret.

When something remarkable happens and bureaucrats take it for only a nuisance, it is often stripped of whatever mystery it may hold. The awesome becomes common. Joe Davis, park manager at Honeyman Dunes State Park, adjacent to the stranding, was charged by the state with getting rid of the whales. He said he didn't take a moment to wonder at the mystery of it.

If ethical problems beset scientists, and mystical considerations occupied other onlookers, a set of concerns more prosaic confronted the police and the Oregon Parks Department. On Sunday night, June 17, police arrested a man in a camouflage suit caught breaking teeth out of a whale's jaw with a hammer and chisel. That night (and the next, and the next) people continued to play games with the police. The Parks Department, for its part, was faced with the disposal of five hundred tons of whale flesh that county environmental and health authorities said they couldn't burn—the solution to the problem at Playa San Rafael—and scientists said couldn't be buried. If buried, the carcasses would become hard envelopes of rotting flesh, the internal organs would liquefy and leach out onto the beach, and winter storms would uncover the whole mess.

This controversy, the public-health question, what to do about excessive numbers of press people, and concern over who was going to pay the bill (the Forest Service had donated tools, vehicles, and labor, but two bulldozers had had to be hired, at a hundred dollars and sixty dollars an hour) precipitated a meeting in Florence on Tuesday morning, June 19. A Forest Service employee, who asked not to be identified, thought the pressures that led to the meeting marked a difference between those who came to the beach out of compassion and genuine interest and those for whom it was "only a headache."

The principal issue, after an agreement was reached to burn the whales, then bury them, was who was going to pay. The state was reluctant; the scientists were impoverished. (It would be months before Mate would begin to recover $5,000 of his own money advanced to pay for equipment, transportation, and bulldozer time. "No one wants to fund work that's finished," Mate observed sardonically.) Commercial firms were averse to donating burning materials, or even transportation for them; G.P. Excavating of Florence did reduce rental fees on its bulldozers by about one-third and "broke even" after paying its operators.

The state finally took responsibility for the disposal and assumed the $25,000 cleanup bill, but it wanted to hear nothing about science's wish to salvage skeletons—it wanted the job finished.* Arrangements were made to

*Three months later on September 6, 1979, an eighty-five-foot female blue whale washed ashore in Northern California. Ensuing argument over responsibility for disposal prevented scientists from going near the whale until September 13, by which time it had been severely battered on the rocks and vandalized.

bring in a crew of boys from the Young Adult Conservation Corps, and the Forest Service, always, it seemed, amenable, agreed to donate several barrels of Alumagel, a napalmlike substance.

It was further decided to ban the public from the beach during the burning, for health and safety reasons. Only the disposal crews, scientists, police, and selected press would be admitted. The criterion for press admittance was possession of "a legitimate press card."

THE ROLE of the press at such events is somewhat predictable. They will repeatedly ask the same, obvious questions; they will often know little of the science involved; occasionally they will intimidate and harass in order to ascertain (or assign) blame. An upper-level Forest Service employee accused the press of asking "the most uninteresting and intimidating kinds of questions." A State Parks employee felt the press fostered dissension over who was going to pay for the disposal. He was also angry with newspaper people for ignoring "the human side," the fact that many state police troopers worked long hours of overtime, and that Forest Service employees performed a number of menial tasks in an emotionally charged environment of rotting flesh. "After a week of sixteen-hour days, your nerves are raw, you stink, you just want to get away from these continual questions."

In the press's defense, the people who objected most were those worried about criticism of their own performance and those deeply frustrated by the trivialization of the event. The press—probing, perhaps inexpertly—made people feel no more than their own misgivings.

The publisher of the local *Siuslaw News*, Paul Holman, said before it was over that the whale stranding had become a nuisance. When police closed the road to the beach a man in a stateside truck began ferrying people the four and a half miles to the whales for a dollar each. And a dollar back. The local airport, as well as tourist centers offering seaplane rides, were doing a "land-office business" in flyovers. Gas station operators got tired of telling tourists how to get to the beach. The Florence City Hall was swamped with calls about the burning, one from a man who was afraid his horses would be killed by the fallout on his pasture. Dune-buggy enthusiasts were angry at whale people who for two days blocked access to their hill-climbing area.

Whatever its interest, the press was largely gone by Monday afternoon. As the burning and burying commenced, the number of interested scientists also thinned. By Wednesday there were only about thirty people left on the beach. Bob Adams, acting director of the Lane Regional Air Pollution Authority, was monitoring the smoke. Neal Langbehn of the National Marine Fisheries Service stood guard over a pile of plastic-wrapped sperm whale jaws. Michael Graybill led a team flensing out skulls. The state fretted over a way to keep the carcasses burning. (It would finally be done with thousands of automobile and truck tires, cordwood, diesel fuel, and

Alumagel.) As Mate watched he considered the threshold of boredom in people, and mourned the loss, among other things, of forty-one sperm whale skeletons.

A journalist, one of the last two or three, asked somebody to take her picture while she stood with a small poodle in her arms in front of the burning pits.

As is often the case with such events, what is salvaged is as much due to goodwill as it is to expertise. The Forest Service was widely complimented for helping, and Stafford Owen, the acting area ranger at the agency's Oregon Dunes National Recreation Area during the incident, tried to say why: "Most of us aren't highly educated people. We have had to work at a variety of things all our lives—operating a chain saw, repairing a truck engine, running a farm. We had the skills these doctors and scientists needed."

A soft-spoken colleague, Gene Large, trying to elaborate but not to make too much of himself, said, "I don't think the scientists had as much knowledge [of large mammalian anatomy] as I did. When it came to it, I had to show some of them where the ribs were." After a moment, Large said, "Trying to cut those whales open with a chain saw was like trying to slaughter a beef with a pen knife." "I didn't enjoy any part of it," Large said of the dismembering with chain saws and winches. "I think the older you get, the more sensitive you get."

He mentioned an older friend who walked away from a dead, fifteen-foot, near-term fetus being lifted out of a gutted whale, and for a time wouldn't speak.

ON WEDNESDAY AFTERNOON the whales were ignited in pits at the foot of the foredune. As they burned they were rendered, and when their oil caught fire they began to boil in it. The seething roar was muffled by a steady onshore breeze; the oily black smoke drifted southeast over the dunes, over English beach grass and pearly everlasting, sand verbena, and the purple flowers of beach pea, green leaves of sweet clover, and the bright yellow blooms of the monkey flower. It thinned until it disappeared against a weak-blue sky.

While fire cracked the blubber of one-eyed, jawless carcasses, a bulldozer the size of a two-car garage grunted in a trench being dug to the north for the last of them. These were still sprawled at the water's edge. Up close, the black, blistered skin, bearing scars of knives and gouging fingernails, looked like the shriveled surface of a pond evaporated beneath a summer sun. Their gray-blue innards lay about on the sand like bags of discarded laundry. Their purple tongues were wedged in retreat in their throats. Spermaceti oil dripped from holes in their heads, solidifying in the wind to stand in translucent stalagmites twenty inches high. Around them were tidal pools opaque with coagulated blood and, beyond, a pink surf.

As far as I know, no novelist, no historian, no moral philosopher, no scholar of Melville, no rabbi, no painter, no theologian had been on the beach. No one had thought to call them or to fly them in. At the end they would not have been allowed past the barricades.

The whales made a sound, someone had said, like the sound a big fir makes breaking off the stump just as the saw is pulled away. A thin screech.

# Children in the Woods

WHEN I WAS A CHILD growing up in the San Fernando Valley in California, a trip into Los Angeles was special. The sensation of movement from a rural area into an urban one was sharp. On one of these charged occasions, walking down a sidewalk with my mother, I stopped suddenly, caught by a pattern of sunlight trapped in a spiraling imperfection in a windowpane. A stranger, an elderly woman in a cloth coat and a dark hat, spoke out spontaneously, saying how remarkable it is that children notice these things.

I have never forgotten the texture of this incident.

Whenever I recall it I am moved not so much by any sense of my young self but by a sense of responsibility toward children, knowing how acutely I was affected in that moment by that woman's words. The effect, for all I know, has lasted a lifetime.

Now, years later, I live in a rain forest in western Oregon, on the banks of a mountain river in relatively undisturbed country, surrounded by 150-foot-tall Douglas firs, delicate deer-head orchids, and clearings where wild berries grow. White-footed mice and mule deer, mink and coyote move through here. My wife and I do not have children, but children we know, or children whose parents we are close to, are often here. They always want to go into the woods. And I wonder what to tell them.

In the beginning, years ago, I think I said too much. I spoke with an encyclopedic knowledge of the names of plants or the names of birds passing through in season. Gradually I came to say less. After a while the only words I spoke, beyond answering a question or calling attention quickly to the slight difference between a sprig of red cedar and a sprig of incense cedar, were to elucidate single objects.

I remember once finding a fragment of a raccoon's jaw in an alder thicket. I sat down alongside the two children with me and encouraged them to find out who this was—with only the three teeth still intact in a piece of the animal's maxilla to guide them. The teeth told by their shape and placement what this animal ate. By a kind of visual extrapolation its size became clear. There were other clues, immediately present, which told, with what I could add of climate and terrain, how this animal lived, how its broken jaw came to be lying here. Raccoon, they surmised. And tiny tooth marks along the bone's broken edge told of a mouse's hunger for calcium.

We set the jaw back and went on.

If I had known more about raccoons, finer points of osteology, we might have guessed more: say, whether it was male or female. But what we deduced was all we needed. Hours later, the maxilla, lost behind us in the detritus of the forest floor, continued to effervesce. It was tied faintly to all else we spoke of that afternoon.

In speaking with children who might one day take a permanent interest in natural history—as writers, as scientists, as filmmakers, as anthropologists—I have sensed that an extrapolation from a single fragment of the whole is the most invigorating experience I can share with them. I think children know that nearly anyone can learn the names of things; the impression made on them at this level is fleeting. What takes a lifetime to learn, they comprehend, is the existence and substance of myriad relationships: it is these relationships, not the things themselves, that ultimately hold the human imagination.

The brightest children, it has often struck me, are fascinated by metaphor—with what is shown in the set of relationships bearing on the raccoon, for example, to lie quite beyond the raccoon. In the end, you are trying to make clear to them that everything found at the edge of one's senses—the high note of the winter wren, the thick perfume of propolis that drifts downwind from spring willows, the brightness of wood chips scattered by beaver—that all this fits together. The indestructibility of these associations conveys a sense of permanence that nurtures the heart, that cripples one of the most insidious of human anxieties, the one that says, you do not belong here, you are unnecessary.

Whenever I walk with a child, I think how much I have seen disappear in my own life. What will there be for this person when he is my age? If he senses something ineffable in the landscape, will I know enough to encourage it?—to somehow show him that, yes, when people talk about violent death, spiritual exhilaration, compassion, futility, final causes, they are drawing on forty thousand years of human meditation on *this*—as we embrace Douglas firs, or stand by a river across whose undulating back we skip stones, or dig out a camas bulb, biting down into a taste so much wilder than last night's potatoes.

The most moving look I ever saw from a child in the woods was on a mud bar by the footprints of a heron. We were on our knees, making handprints beside the footprints. You could feel the creek vibrating in the silt and sand. The sun beat down heavily on our hair. Our shoes were soaking wet. The look said: I did not know until now that I needed someone much older to confirm this, the feeling I have of life here. I can now grow older, knowing it need never be lost.

The quickest door to open in the woods for a child is the one that leads to the smallest room, by knowing the name each thing is called. The door that leads to the cathedral is marked by a hesitancy to speak at all, rather to encourage by example a sharpness of the senses. If one speaks it should only be to say, as well as one can, how wonderfully all this fits together, to indicate what a long, fierce peace can derive from this knowledge.

# The Lives of Seals

IN MY HEAVY CLOTHING it is hard to move with any grace. I bend over awkwardly to retrieve shells from a nameless island at the edge of the Arctic Ocean, with an intention that is clear but for reasons difficult to articulate. At my feet are a startling variety—residue of the lives of surf clams, Greenland cockles, razor clams, whelks. Seeded among the shells are bits of shattered bone, an occasional tooth—residue of Eskimo hunting camps. In the wind is the smell of decay; a beach-cast walrus lies a hundred yards away where the Chukchi Sea rasps and hammers at the sand. I lay back into its frozen pocket on the beach a primitive tool—seal bone, weathered smooth as polished wood, carved by hands long dead.

I pick up three or four of the most striking shells and cross back to the far side of the barrier island, where two friends wait. The lagoon is called Kasegaluk. In pale, flat light, against the memory of beating our way in here through heavy seas in a small boat, its still waters seem apparitional. The gray heads of spotted seals break its surface full of curiosity, then disappear abruptly, a snap of the fingers.

We sit back against a piece of driftwood with a simple lunch, a meal prepared that morning by people working on an oceanographic research vessel now waiting several miles to sea in deeper water. A mother ship. As isolated as we are on this barrier island, beneath somber skies, we feel attached, agreeably, to the ship. To some of those aboard what we are about to do is enigmatic, nearly arcane—or simply wrong, for we are about to take the lives of these seals. But other threads draw us together, the biologists I am with, myself, the ship's crew. It is for the people on the ship that I have picked up the shells. We eat the sandwiches now, the thick homemade soup prepared for us; at the end of the day the deck crew will snatch us again from the dead-cold water. If what we are about to do is to have any transcendent meaning it must in the end be meaningful to these cooks and mates and engineers. It must make sense not only to those acquainted with marine science, to those who comprehend the threat that oil development poses to life in these waters; it must also be comprehensible to the ones who clearly perceive only that certain shells are stunningly beautiful. That, at least, is the ideal of this kind of science—to enhance the life, somehow, of each human being.

On this particular fall day, as we prepare to kill the seals, the ideal is only vaguely with us. It is as distant as the violent image of an oil blowout, or the racket of automobiles stifled in traffic, or the slick-sell commerce of politics. We eat here in a remote and vast stillness, watching the seals appear and disappear in the glassy water; the moral ambiguities of such field science, even when death comes at the hands of decent and thoughtful men, are a perpetual ache.

I would like to pretend that the seals don't die. But they do. To pretend no animal dies in our efforts to take the measure of life—here at this lagoon, so the country can develop its energy reserves—is to ignore the responsibility inherent in committing the act.

No one thinks this out very well. Sipping my coffee, I wonder more about the rough water beyond the barrier island, whether the seas will come down before late afternoon and make the trip back easier. Safer. And I stare at the shells resting on a strip of wind-crusted snow by my foot, which glow with a pearling light.

THIS PART of the Alaskan coast, southwest of Icy Cape, is only vaguely known to biologists. The two I am with, Lloyd Lowry and Bob Nelson of the Alaska

Department of Fish and Game, have spent the past month (and several months in the previous year) conducting a marine mammal reconnaissance along these coasts and examining food-chain relationships in the nearshore waters. The daily work entails bottom trawls and vertical plankton tows, collecting seals to examine stomach contents and to determine general state of health, and pinpointing areas habitually used by seals to rest and feed. The work is rote, but never monotonous. Each sampling of the water column with a fine-mesh, half-meter-wide net brings up a rich, translucent, writhing mass of copepods and other zooplankton—we hold them up in clear plastic Whirl-Paks against the light of the sky and marvel at the radiance and energy of this life. From otter trawls at five-, ten-, and fifteen-meter depths come the creatures that feed on this zooplankton—shrimps, mysids and euphausids, crabs and sculpins, eelpout, arctic and saffron cod, Alaska plaice, yellowfin sole, and dozens of others. And from the stomachs of seals come the remains of these creatures, and with that some crude sense of the food web here. The time and place of the trawls, the number of seals feeding at a particular lagoon entrance, air temperatures, water temperatures—everything is written down in a waterproof notebook. In the evening these raw notes are refined and in a shipboard laboratory a more thorough analysis of the trawls is made. Seal stomach contents and certain internal organs and representative organisms from the trawls and plankton tows are prepared for later analysis.

The work of Lowry and Nelson and their colleagues is funded by the Outer Continental Shelf Environmental Assessment Program and meant to complement the work of other biologists, geologists, ornithologists, and ecologists to create a reasonably clear picture of this region, one that, among other things, will be substantial enough to direct the process of offshore oil and mineral exploration along the least harmful course.

Such abstract ideas, the uncluttered logic of it all, seem impossible and amusing on this barrier island. Logistical support here is complicated and horrendously expensive. The work is arduous, the weather frequently harsh, and on some days we shoot poorly or struggle with fouled nets and broken lines and have nothing to show. Our daily operations are conducted from a twenty-foot open boat with outboard engines. It must be attended to each day. Freezing temperatures, salt spray, the abrading sea ice, and rough water exact a toll; combined with cutting snow squalls and navigating in dense fog banks these impediments also take a toll on us. Our daily regimen of inspection and repair is strict, and includes ourselves, an attentiveness to our sense of humor and perspective.

Before the three of us came aboard the NOAA ship *Oceanographer* at Barrow, Alaska, a rumor was circulating on board that several marine biologists—I was a writer accompanying them—were going to be killing seals every day and hauling them back to the ship to butcher on the fantail. This news disturbed some members of the crew, who thought carefully about their objections to the killing and later expressed them. Why, they asked, did the seals have to die?

The second evening aboard ship, Lowry—chief scientist in a group that also included two ornithologists, a woman studying walrus biology, and a technician servicing water-current meters along the coast—addressed the crew. He explained how the work would be carried out from the small boat every day; he spoke about trophic, or food web, relationships and their complexity; and he indicated how these data could be used to guide oil and mineral development. He said nothing about the killing of seals beyond the fact that seals would be "collected" as part of this process. He urged the crew and officers, finally, to visit the lab whenever they wished and to ask the scientists about anything that was on their minds. Anyone who wanted to help, he said, in the sometimes tedious business of sorting the contents of the trawls (for which we were using Russian taxonomic guides, there being no suitable American guides for that part of the world) would be welcome. Lowry spoke extemporaneously, ingenuously, without self-importance or scientific distance. In the days that followed people visited the lab with growing frequency.

Most of the crew aboard the *Oceanographer* were based in Seattle. Few had ever been to the Arctic Ocean. Over a period of weeks their, and our, cumulative experience of the region—immense flocks of migrating waterfowl, the open pack ice, pods of feeding gray whales, the long lingering of orange and purple light at dusk, the piggish odor of walrus, the sudden appearance of a polar bear in the water on a foggy morning—all this nourished a sense of the biological richness of the region. And its separateness. These feelings were enhanced in the lab. People marveled at the variety of the species the trawls brought up, at the diversity of anatomical design, at the vitality of an ocean they knew to be frigid, even at its sunlit surface.

A fragile camaraderie began to grow in these evening conversations with the crew, a sense of affinity, a sense of the privilege of exotic circumstances. One or two of the ship's engineers took to visiting the lab regularly to help sort specimens. The ship's carpenter, a man with many years at sea in a variety of ships, became fascinated with the fine details of seal anatomy. In this way, some of what was learned each day (and a certain amount of what was collected, for shrimp often ended up in the ship's kitchen) found its way out of the laboratory.

One can be fooled by the casualness of such moments, by the informality of the conversations, the exchanges. As certain crew members became more adept at distinguishing taxonomic details, however, you could see that they carried themselves somewhat differently. And the desires that some scientists have—that their work be appreciated, that they be understood simply as other human beings trying to grasp the meaning of some part of the universe—those desires were also met in the laboratory each evening.

Because we do not readily share the private reaches of ourselves with each other, little of the pleasure we take in such encounters is ever articulated. During those weeks, however, in the evenings when I spoke with members of the crew, I discovered the far side of the rumor that had been there in the beginning, that faceless men whose life was killing seals were coming aboard. I sensed, when I stood in the companionway chatting with a Filipino steward about the taste of shrimp, or discussed seal biology with a ship's technician, or listened to an engineer explain, ardently and with confidence, the operation of the Fairbanks Morse engines that drove the ship, I sensed in those moments an aura of mutual regard. The dignity of each person's task, the dignity of their occupations, emerged.

The intuition one has that these things are present is as intangible as light. The feeling reached me directly and suddenly when a ship's officer, a man always somewhat aloof, stopped abruptly in a stairwell and said self-consciously that they had never had a finer group of scientists aboard. Or when a member of the crew beamed with surprise and pleasure at our remembering to bring back one of the common shells of the barrier beach. On our last day a sort of wistful exuberance pervaded the ship; something subtly affirming was so obviously over.

I know of few grounds more delicate to speak of than these. The hope of each human being to have a sense of value in his or her life is squarely before you. The desire to carry out fatal work honorably. The dream of fathoming the biology of seals. The notion of a rational and humane development of energy in the Arctic. The wordless euphoria in a person touched by the fecundity and resoluteness of the natural world, the vague belief that one is, or could be, a part of this. Such hopes are too deeply wished to be expressed; we convey them obliquely in our gestures, in our cultivation of an atmosphere of tolerance.

THE AFTERNOON I sat on the beach at Kasegaluk Lagoon, at an ancient Eskimo hunting site, eating food prepared by stewards for people they had come to like, I thought hard about killing seals. I understood some of the extenuating circumstances, and that, ironically, environmentalists would have these data to stand on in a court of law. But I had no finished answer. I stood uncomfortable, like so many, in the middle of the question.

We took their lives with as much dispatch and skill and respect as possible. Every bit of useful information was carefully written down, all the measurements and observations. We took the contents of the stomachs and various organs. And we let what remained slide quietly into the sea. We washed the blood from our clothes and off the boat. We never came back to the ship with signs of blood, not because we wished to obscure the seals' deaths but because it would have been so abjectly callow. One young woman, initially upset about the seal killings, said that though she came to understand the context and so would not condemn it, she would not countenance it. It was out of respect for such opinion that we brought no obvious sign of death back. From such small considerations, and with the hard thought of moral philosophers, it is possible to imagine that people will find some better answer to the animals' deaths than that they must die for the sake of an advancing civilization.

As a journalist I have listened to biologists complain that their work is used by politicians to advance technologies they don't believe in. I've been with Eskimo hunters who are dumbfounded by what people say about their way of life, that it is barbaric because it includes the hunting of animals. And aboard the *Oceanographer* I heard officers speculate about the propriety of killing animals for science, and members of a deck crew wonder that any sense could be made of a churning mass of animals dying in a trawl net. In each of these moments you could hear someone struggling to grasp another's point of view, to assess it.

One can adopt any of several attitudes toward what took place between a scientific party and a ship's crew aboard a research vessel one fall in the Chukchi Sea, precisely because what happened was without design. You could be cynical and say that the atmosphere aboard ships is romantic. You could be circumspect and say it is naive to believe that any such goodwill can extend very far beyond the moment. You could be grave and say that beside the death of seals, let alone copepods in a Whirl-Pak of formalin, any notion of a redeeming introspection or ultimate value is an evasion, a gloss, worthless to consider. But in each of these ways you crush something precious, as precious as knowledge of the behavior of pi-mesons or the orders of human personality. And you deny something fundamental: our acts, the consequences of our seemingly dissimilar lives, are irrevocably intertwined.

The marine survey of the Alaskan coast that Lowry and the others conducted will find its way to the desks of industrialists and environmentalists and scientists and lawyers, and they will discuss what is to be done at places like Kasegaluk Lagoon. And if they drill for oil at Kasegaluk, in land that has known only hunting and fishing camps for eight thousand years, and the seals and the polar bears and the nesting birds go away, it may be argued that nothing much has changed. But it will have changed. The members of a scientific party and the people aboard a ship will know it changed, and that they had a part in it. And they will tell their children, and their neighbors. And they will know one, inescapable thing—the hard questions about death and propriety and human acquisition never go away. And that you have to stay far into the night to comprehend, let alone answer them. And that in the end it is madness to answer them as though everyone lived alone, to answer them as if there were no seals.

# *Searching for Ancestors*

I AM LYING ON MY BACK in northern Arizona. The sky above, the familiar arrangement of stars at this particular latitude on a soft June evening, is comforting. I reach out from my sleeping bag, waiting for sleep, and slowly brush the Kaibab Plateau, a grit of limestone 230 million years old. A slight breeze, the settling air at dusk, carries the pungent odor of blooming cliffrose.

Three of us sleep in this clearing, on the west rim of Marble Canyon above the Colorado River. Two archaeologists and myself, out hunting for tangible remains of the culture called Anasazi. The Anasazi abandoned this particular area for good around A.D. 1150, because of drought, deteriorating trade alliances, social hostilities—hard to say now. But while they flourished, both here and farther to the east in the austere beauty of canyons called de Chelly and Chaco, they represented an apotheosis in North American culture, like the Hopewell of Ohio or the horse-mounted Lakota of the plains in the last century.

In recent years the Anasazi have come to signify prehistoric Indians in the same way the Lakota people have been made to stand for all historic Indians. Much has been made of the "mystery" of their disappearance. And perhaps because they seem "primitive," they are too easily thought of as an uncomplicated people with a comprehensible culture. It is not, and they are not. We know some things about them. From the start they were deft weavers, plaiting even the utensils they cooked with. Later they became expert potters and masons, strongly influencing cultures around them. They were clever floodwater farmers. And astronomers; not as sophisticated as the Maya, but knowledgeable enough to pinpoint the major celestial events, to plant and celebrate accordingly.

They were intimate with the landscape, a successful people. Around A.D. 1300 they slipped through a historical crevice to emerge (as well as we know) as the people now called Hopi and Zuni, and the pueblo peoples of the Rio Grande Valley—Keres, Tiwa, Tewa.

On a long, dry June day like this, hundreds of tourists wander in fascination at Mesa Verde and Pueblo

Bonito; and I am out here on the land the Anasazi once walked—here with two people who squat down to look closely at the land itself before they say anything about its former inhabitants. Even then they are reticent. We are camped here amid the indigenous light siennas and dark umbers, the wild red of ripe prickly pear fruit, the dull silver of buffalo berry bushes, the dark, luminous green of a field of snakegrass.

We inquire after the Anasazi. Because we respect the spiritual legacy of their descendants, the Hopi. Because of the contemporary allure of Taos. Because in our own age we are "killing the hidden waters" of the Southwest, and these were a people who took swift, resourceful advantage of whatever water they could find. Because of the compelling architecture of their cliff dwellings, the stunning placement of their homes in the stone walls of Betatakin, as if set in the mouth of an enormous wave or at the bottom of a towering cumulus cloud. We make the long automobile trip to Hovenweep or the hike into Tsegi Canyon to gaze at Keet Seel. It is as though we believed *here* is a good example, here are stories to get us through the night.

SOME EIGHT THOUSAND years ago, after the decline of the Folsom and Clovis hunters, whose spearpoints are still found in the crumbling arroyos of New Mexico, a culture we know very little about emerged in the Great Basin. Archaeologists call it simply the Desert Culture. Some two thousand years ago, while Rome was engaged in the Macedonian wars, a distinct group of people emerged from this complex. They were called Anasazi from the Navajo *anaasází*, meaning "someone's ancestors." Their culture first appeared in the Four Corners country, where Utah, Arizona, New Mexico, and Colorado meet. By this time (A.D. 1) they were already proficient weavers and basketmakers, living a mixed agricultural hunter-gatherer life and dwelling in small groups in semisubterranean houses. Archaeologists call this period, up to about A.D. 700, the Basket Maker Period. It was followed by a Pueblo Period (A.D. 700–1598), during which time the Anasazi built the great cliff and pueblo dwellings by which most of us know them.

Archaeologists divide the Anasazi occupation geographically into three contemporary traditions—Kayenta, Chaco, and Mesa Verde. Here, where I have rolled my sleeping bag out this June evening, Kayenta Anasazi lived, in an area of about ten thousand square miles bounded by the Henry Mountains in Utah, the Little Colorado River to the south, Grand Canyon to the west, and Chinle Wash, near the New Mexico border, to the east. This part of the Anasazi country has long been of interest to Robert Euler, the research anthropologist at Grand Canyon National Park. He lies quietly now a few yards away from me, in the night shadow of a large juniper tree. From here, at the lip of Marble Canyon and the old edge of Anasazi territory, amid the very same plants the Anasazi took such perceptive advantage of—threads of the yucca leaf to be made into snares; the soft, shreddy bark of the cliffrose to absorb the flow of blood; delicate black seeds of rice grass to eat—from here, with the aid of an observer like Euler, it is possible to imagine who these people might have been, to make some cautious surmise about them and the meaning they may have for us, who wistfully regard them now as mysterious and vanished, like the Eskimo curlew.

We go toward sleep this evening—Euler, a colleague named Trinkle Jones, and myself—restless with the bright, looming memory of a granary we have located today, a small storage structure below a cliff edge that has been visited only by violet-green swallows and pack rats since its Anasazi owners walked away some eight hundred years ago. It is like a piece of quartz in the mind.

IN A QUIET CORNER of the national park's health clinic on the south rim of the Grand Canyon, an entire wall of Euler's modest office is covered by books. A small slip of paper there reads:

> These are not books, lumps of lifeless paper, but *minds* alive on the shelves. From each of them goes out its own voice, as inaudible as the streams of sound conveyed day and night by electric waves beyond the range of our physical hearing; and just as the touch of a button on our set will fill the room with music, so by taking down one of these volumes and opening it, one can call into range the far

> distant voice in time and space, and hear it speaking to us, mind to mind, heart to heart.
>
> GILBERT HIGHET

Highet was a classics scholar. The words reflect his respect for the ideas of other cultures, other generations, and for the careful deliberations of trained minds. Euler is in this mold; keen and careful, expert in his field, but intent on fresh insight. At fifty-seven, with an ironic wit, willing to listen attentively to the ideas of an amateur, graciously polite, he is the sort of man you wish had taught you in college.

Of the Anasazi he says: "It is relatively easy to see *what* they did, but why did they do these things? What were their values? What were the fundamental relationships between their institutions—their politics, economics, religion? All we can do is infer, from what we pick up on the ground."

To elucidate the Anasazi, Euler and his colleagues have taken several ingenious steps in recent years. In the 1920s a man named Andrew Douglass pioneered a system of dating called dendrochronology. By comparing borings from timbers used in Anasazi dwellings, Douglass and his successors eventually constructed a continuous record of tree-ring patterns going back more than two thousand years. The measurements are so precise that archaeologists can, for instance, tell that a room in a particular dwelling in Chaco Canyon was roofed over in the spring or summer of 1040 with timbers cut in the fall or winter of 1039.

Using dendrochronology as a parallel guide in time, archaeologists have been able to corroborate and assemble long sequences of pottery design. With the aid of radiocarbon dating, obsidian hydration dating, and a technique called thermoluminescence, they have pinned down dates for cooking fires and various tools. By determining kinds of fossil pollens and their ratios to each other, palynologists have reconstructed former plant communities, shedding light on human diets at the time and establishing a history of weather patterns.

With such a convergence of dates and esoteric information, archaeologists can figure out when a group of people were occupying a certain canyon, what sort of meals they were eating, what kind of animals and plants were present there, and how they were adapting their farming methods and living patterns to cope with, say, several years of heavy rainfall. With more prosaic techniques—simple excavation and observation—much more becomes clear: details and artifacts of personal adornment; locally traded items (beans and squash for tanned deerskin) and distant trade patterns (turquoise for abalone shell beads from California or copper bells from Mexico); and prevalent infirmities and diseases (arthritis, iron-deficiency anemia).

As much as one can learn, however—the Anasazi were a short people with straight black hair, who domesticated turkeys for a supply of feathers, which they carefully wrapped around string and wove together to make blankets—the information seems hollow when you are standing in the cool silence of one of the great kivas at Mesa Verde. Or staring at the stone that soars like a cathedral vault above White House Ruin in Canyon de Chelly. Or turning an Anasazi flute over in your hands. The analytic tools of science can obscure the fact that these were a people. They had an obvious and pervasive spiritual and aesthetic life, as well as clothing made of feathers and teeth worn down by the grit in their cornmeal. Their abandoned dwellings and ceremonial kivas would seem to make this clear. This belief by itself—that they were a people of great spiritual strength—makes us want to know them, to understand what they understood.

THE DAY EULER AND JONES discovered the intact granary, with its handful of tiny corncobs, I was making notes about the plants and animals we had encountered and trying to envision how water fell and flowed away over this parched land. Euler had told me the area we were traversing was comparable to what the Anasazi had known when they were here, though it was a little drier now. Here then was buffalo berry, which must have irritated their flesh with the white powder beneath its leaves, as it did mine. And apache plume, from whose stout twigs the Anasazi made arrows. And a species of sumac, from the fruits of which they made a sweet lemonade. Dogbane, from whose fibrous stems they wove sandals, proof against scorpions, cactus spines, and the other sharp and pointed edges of this country.

One afternoon I came on the remains of a mule

deer killed by a mountain lion and thought the Anasazi, eminently practical, must have availed themselves of such meat. And I considered the sheltered, well-stocked dwellings of the pack rat, who may have indicated to the newly arrived Anasazi the value of providence and storage.

Such wandering is like an interrogation of the landscape, trying by means of natural history and analog to pry loose from it a sense of a people who would be intimate with it—knowledgeable of the behavior of its ground and surface water, its seven-year cycle of piñon nut production, the various subtle euphonies of whirring insects, bumblebees, and hummingbirds on a June afternoon—a people reflective of its order.

Euler stood by me at one point when I asked about a particular plant—did they parch, very carefully, the tiny seeds of this desert plume in fiber baskets over their fires?—and said that their botany was so good they probably made use of everything they could digest.

They made mistakes, too, if you want to call them that: farmed one area too intensively and ruined the soil; cut down too many trees with their stone axes for housing and firewood and abetted erosion; overhunted. But they survived. They lived through long droughts and took advantage of years of wetness to secure their future. One of the great lessons of the Anasazi is one of the great lessons of all aboriginal peoples, of human ecology in general: Individuals die—of starvation, disease, and injury; but the population itself—resourceful, practical, determined—carries on through nearly everything. Their indomitable fierceness is as attractive as the power we imagine concentrated in their kivas.

With the Anasazi, however, you must always turn back and look at the earth—the earth they farmed and hunted and gathered fruits and nuts and seeds upon—and to the weather. The Anasazi responded resourcefully and decisively to the earth and the weather that together made their land. If they were sometimes victims of their environment through drought or epidemic disease, they were more often on excellent terms with it. Given a slight advantage, as they were about A.D. 600 and again about A.D. 1150, when food was abundant at the peak of the Southwest's 550-year moisture cycle, their culture flourished. Around A.D. 600 they developed pottery, the cultivated bean, and the bow and arrow. In the bean was an important amino acid, lysine, not available in the corn they cultivated. Their diet improved dramatically. By 1150 the Anasazi were building pueblos with three-story, freestanding walls, and their crafts were resurgent during this "classic" period. We can only wonder what might have happened at the next climatic, in 1700—but by then the hostile Spanish were among them.

The rise and fall of Anasazi fortunes in time with the weather patterns of the region is clear to most historians. What is not clear is how much of a role weather played in the final retreat of the Anasazi in A.D. 1300 from areas they had long occupied—Mesa Verde, southern Black Mesa, Chaco Canyon. Toward the end, the Anasazi were building what seem to be defensive structures, but it is unclear against whom they were defending themselves. A good guess is that they were defending themselves against themselves, that this was a period of intense social feuding. The sudden alteration of trading relationships, social and political realignment in the communities, drought—whatever the reasons, the Anasazi departed. Their descendants took up residence along the Rio Grande, near springs on the Hopi mesas, and on tributaries of the Little Colorado where water was more dependable. Here, too, they developed farming techniques that were not so harmful to the land.

FOR MANY in the Southwest today the Anasazi are a vague and nebulous passage in the history of human life. For others, like Euler, they are an intense reflection of the land, a puzzle to be addressed the way a man might try to understand the now-departed curlew. For still others they are a spiritual repository, a mysterious source of strength born of their intimacy with the Colorado Plateau.

To wonder about the Anasazi today at a place like the Grand Canyon is to be humbled—by space and the breadth of time—to find the Anasazi neither remote nor primitive, but transcendent. The English novelist J. B. Priestley once said that if he were an American he would make the final test of whatever men chose to do in art and politics a comparison with this place. He believed that whatever was cheap and ephemeral would be revealed for what it was when stood up against it. Priestley was an intellectual, but he had his finger on an abiding aboriginal truth: If something will not stand up in the land, then it doesn't belong there. It is right that it should die. Most of us are now so far removed from either a practical or an aesthetic intimacy with North America that the land is no longer an arbiter for us. And a haunting sense that this arrangement is somewhat dangerous brings us to stare into the Grand Canyon and to contemplate the utter honesty of the Anasazi's life here.

IN 1906, with some inkling that North America was slowly being stripped of the evidence of its aboriginal life and that a knowledge of such life was valuable, Congress passed a protective Antiquities Act. The impulse in 1979 to pass a much stronger Archaeological Resources Act was different. Spurred on by escalating prices for Anasazi artifacts, thieves had been systematically looting sites for commercial gain. The trend continues. A second serious current threat to this human heritage is the small number of tourists who, sometimes innocently, continue to destroy structures, walk off with artifacts, and deface petroglyphs. More ominously, the national parks and monuments where most Anasazi sites are now found operate on such restricted budgets that they are unable to adequately inventory, let alone protect, these cultural resources.

Of the Grand Canyon's two thousand or more aboriginal sites only three have been both excavated and stabilized. Of its 1.2 million acres, 500,000 have never even been visited by an archaeologist or historian. In the summer of 1981 an unknown person or persons pushed in the wall of an Anasazi granary on the Colorado River at the mouth of Nankoweap Canyon, one of the most famous sites in the park.

The sites, which people come so far every year to visit, are more vulnerable every year.

On a helicopter reconnaissance in September 1981, part of a long-term project to locate and describe aboriginal sites in the park, Trinkle Jones found what she thought was a set of untouched ruins in the west rim of Marble Canyon. It was almost a year before she and Euler could get there to record them, on a trip on which I accompanied them.

EULER IS GLAD to get out into the country, into the canyons that have been the focus of his work since 1960. He moves easily through the juniper-piñon savannahs, around the face of a cliff and along narrow trails with a practiced stride, examining bits of stone and brush. His blue eyes often fill with wonder when he relates bits of Anasazi history, his right hand sometimes turning slowly in the air as he speaks, as if he were showing you a rare fruit. He tells me one night that he reveres the land, that he thinks about his own footprints impressed in the soil and on the plants, how long before there will be no trace.

Euler is a former college president, an author and editor, has been on several university faculties and a codirector of the Black Mesa Archaeological Project, working one step ahead of Peabody Coal's drag buckets. The Park Service, so severely hampered by its humiliating lack of funds, is fortunate, at least, to be able to retain such men.

The granaries Jones found prove, indeed, to be untouched. Over a period of several days we map and describe nine new ruins. The process is somewhat mechanical, but we each take pleasure in the simple tasks. As the Anasazi had a complicated culture, so have we. We are takers of notes, measurers of stone, examiners of fragments in the dust. We search for order in chaos wherever we go. We worry over what is lost. In our best moments we remember to ask ourselves what it is we are doing, whom we are benefiting by these acts. One of the great dreams of man must be to find some place between the extremes of nature and civilization where it is possible to live without regret.

I LIE IN MY SLEEPING BAG, staring up at the Big Dipper and other familiar stars. It is surprisingly cool. The moon has risen over the land of the Navajo nation to the east. Bats flutter overhead, swooping after moths. We are the only people, I reflect, who go to such lengths to record and preserve the past. In the case of the Anasazi it is not even our own past. Until recently Indians distrusted this process. When Andrew Douglass roamed the Southwest looking for house timbers to core to establish his dendrochronologies, he was required to trade bolts of velveteen for the privilege and to close off every drill hole with a piece of turquoise.

I roll on my side and stare out into the canyon's abyss. I think of the astonishing variety of insects and spiders I have seen today—stinkbugs inverted in cactus flowers, butterflies, tiny biting gnats and exotic red velvet ants, and on the ceiling of an Anasazi granary a very poisonous brown recluse spider. For all the unrelieved tedium there might seem to be in the miles of juniper-piñon savannah, for all the cactus spines, sharp stones, strong light, and imagined strikes of rattlesnakes, the land is replete with creatures, and there is a soft and subtle beauty here. Turn an ash-white mule deer antler over, and its underside, where it has lain against the earth, is flushed rose. Yellow pollen clings to the backs of my hands. Wild grasses roll in the wind, like the manes of horses. It is important to remember that the Anasazi lived in a place, and that the place was very much like the place I lie in tonight.

The Anasazi are a reminder: Human life is fundamentally diverse and finally impenetrable. That we cannot do better than a crude reconstruction of their life on the Colorado Plateau a thousand years ago is probably to our advantage, for it steers us away from presumption and judgment.

I roll over again and look at the brightening stars. How fortunate we all are, I think, to have people like Euler among us, with their long-lived inquiries; to have these bits of the Anasazi Way to provoke our speculation, to humble us in this long and endless struggle to find ourselves in the world.

The slow inhalation of light that is the fall of dusk is now complete. The stars are very bright. I lie there recalling the land as if the Anasazi were something that had once bloomed in it.

# Grown Men

I RETURNED FROM a week of camping in the high desert of eastern Oregon, a respite from the twilight and winter rains on the west side of the Cascade Mountains where I live, to find a letter with a straightforward message, that Odey Cassell was dead.

It had been a year for deaths. My mother had died of cancer in Lenox Hill Hospital in New York. An uncle I was close to died of a heart attack among strangers in the Atlanta airport. I had lost with their fading a sense of family, as though the piers had suddenly gone out from under the veranda of an ancestral southern home and revealed it abandoned. I was brooding over that sense of emptiness when the letter about Odey came, written in Nettie's fine, neat hand.

He had gone unremarkably one morning, wrote his wife, in his own bed in a house he had lived in since he was born in its living room in 1885. I was weary of deaths, but this passing stunned me. I spent the evening trying to answer Nettie's letter, trying half the night to say how grateful I was to have known him.

I first met Odey in the spring of 1964. A friend, Peter, and I drove down from Notre Dame, where I was in school, to spend a week with the Cassells. Their farm lay northeast of Cass, West Virginia, beneath Back Allegheny Mountain on the Greenbrier River. Its cleared fields were cut out square against the hills, in a dense second growth of oak, maple and white pine. Peter had first met them in 1961, when he saw a card on a bulletin board in Cass—"Home cooked meals and overnight, $1 per meal, $1 for bed"—and found his way out to them, to a two-story clapboard house, white paint faded to light gray, a large unpainted barn, a woodshed, split-rail and wire fences, Nettie's garden, and, overhead, a 125-Kv power line that passed through their lives, over chickens, a few cows, twenty-five or thirty sheep, some pigs and their border collie, Topsy.

What Nettie put on her table for a single meal was more than most people saw in three. Farm meals, plain food meant for working people. Tomatoes and green beans, yellow squash, potatoes, carrots and sweet corn. Mutton and ham. Fresh milk, churned butter and honey, fresh bread and biscuits. All of it, save the grains, from the farm.

The guest beds upstairs were hard to match in our minds for comfort: feather mattresses on box springs with layers of quilts and sun-stiffened sheets. Their home was wood-heated; the water system gravity-fed from a stream on a hill behind the house. Hot water ran out of a circulating pipe in a wood stove in the kitchen. A loaded .30/30 leaned against the pale yellow wall by the front door, for bears and feral dogs, for the sake of the sheep.

We went to Odey's farm because it was so different from what we knew, because we were eighteen and sensed adventure in it.

In the evenings Odey would tell stories, dozens of them, on visit after visit, never the same one twice unless he was asked. He drew us in, sitting wide-eyed and silent in his living room. We never heard enough; later we barely understood how to retell them.

Whenever we came we brought him two cans of Prince Albert pipe tobacco and a little Jack Daniel's. Nettie didn't approve of the whiskey. Odey's eyes would sparkle behind his wire-frame glasses, a look of boyish surprise would come over him and he'd affect astonishment and delight at her disapproval. And he'd say, "Well, boys, I declare. . . ." He studied the gifts, turning them slowly in his hands as though they were as exotic for him as ostrich eggs. "Thank you," he would say. He was the first man I knew who was not accustomed to receiving inexpensive gifts.

Odey was slow to begin a session of stories, as the art required, but once under way the range of his historical experience, the touch for revealing detail, his timing and rhythmic pace took you and lulled you. Almost every incident of which he spoke—the time a wounded owl punctured his hand, the way they cut ice on the river with horse-drawn saws—had occurred within twenty miles of the house we sat in. He'd cleared the land around it with his father and a team of oxen before the turn of the century. He'd seen commercial logging for white pine and spruce come and go, and with it the railroad and the town. Cass now supported only a clothespin factory, and in summer rides to a nearby hilltop behind an antique Shay logging engine. In spring the half dozen wheelless cars in vacant lots sat strangling in vines. His children had gone on to become a university professor, a state trooper. Another son, the youngest, had stayed on to help his parents, working part-time in the Green Bank Observatory, nine miles east by foot or thirty by West Virginia mountain road.

At seventy-eight, six-feet-four-inches tall, with hands so large he had to take a doorknob in his fingertips, with physical strokes perfectly measured to whatever work had to be done—splitting wood or winding the stem of his pocket watch—he strode down the road with us on an evening walk at a pace we couldn't catch. And he knew it.

Odey was outsize for us, in part because he hardly made himself the subject of conversation, and we felt this a quality to admire. In the years we visited we heard stories of his prodigious physical strength and his generosity only from friends, neighbors with names like Walter Beverage and Charles Seabolt. It pleased us to think that they thought of him as we did, though to them he was only what they were to him, all of value in that country, neighbors, ones who went way back.

At the time, the largest unexplored cave in West Virginia lay under Odey's land. With the aid of some crude maps made by a U.S. Geological Survey crew, Peter and I went down into its tunnels and caverns, an adventure of self-induced terror and, to be sure, of awesome sights. When we unraveled our stories that evening Odey listened as keenly as we had to him, strengthening the flow of our narrative with a gentle question or two, helping us shape it, though we could not understand this at the time.

We stumbled into rattlesnakes in the nearby hills (he told us once their dens smelled like cucumbers, and he was right); and we watched, stunned, one night from a second-story window as a black bear tore up his sheep pens and most of his cash income for the year. The next morning he fired up the stove, milked the cow and went to work on the sheep.

I don't ever remember getting up earlier than he did.

I learned more than I comprehended at Odey's, about hardware disease in cows and how to shoot crows; about a farmer's life eighty years long, set dead against half as many bitter winters, violent economic loss, forest fires, friends chewed up in farm machinery, and still-born children; about backwoods skills thought unremarkable, and a capacity for improvisation—quick and sharp in men with little income who work alone. He was, of course, like a grandfather to me, in part because I had never known grandfathers. He was orthodox in that he never spoke in our presence of religion or politics. In general, he moved us by his own example toward a respect for people for whatever they might do well, and to recall that different people lived in different ways. I never saw bitterness or resentment in him. Or meanness.

In later years, when I read about Appalachia in books like Harry Caudill's *Night Comes to the Cumberlands* or heard a man like Doc Watson sing of hard lives in the hills, I would think of the thing Odey had given us: we had lived that time like willow shoots with a man rooted in the earth like a tan oak. We had repaired his fences and milked his cows and run his sheep and brought him whiskey; and he had told us well-fetched stories of young ladies met at county fairs, or bear-hunting for meat, and of practical jokes to break the back of a terrible winter, about what he thought were the courtesies and obligations in life, in short to be self-reliant and neighborly, and grateful for what there was. And then he sent us on our way.

Some things Odey said about integrity didn't bloom in me for years. For the most part they came in time.

* * *

THERE WAS another man. During the summers after my sophomore and junior years at Notre Dame, I moved West to work in Wyoming, some of that time with a man in his sixties named Bill Daniels. We cleared forest trails together and I wrangled horses on a few trips on which he was employed as a cook. He took a liking to me. On our days off he took me into places in the Teton Wilderness Area he felt not many men had seen.

At the request of the Museum of Natural History in New York, Bill Daniels had prepared an exhibit on Sheepeater Indians, people banished to the Rocky Mountain ranges by their respective tribes for heinous crimes, people who lived on bighorn sheep the way Plains Indians lived on buffalo. As far as I know, he was the only man around at the time who knew the location of several of their caves and could easily find evidence of their vanished culture. My time with him was less keen and shorter than that with Odey but he introduced me to a perception of America's indigenous people more complex than anything I was later to read about them, and he formed in me a sympathy for mountain men.

I realized later that he saw, without motive or design, to a part of my education that required his attention.

THERE WAS A third man who affected me as much as these two, though years later, a kind of frontier roustabout named Dave Wallace. As a young man he had hunted wolves and coyotes for bounty in North and South Dakota. He later moved to eastern Montana where he worked on cattle ranches and drilled for oil before going north to crew on a commercial fishing boat in the Gulf of Alaska. I met him, crippled by accidents sustained in those and other jobs, living in the southeastern Oregon desert where he was making a living mining and trapping coyotes.

I spent several days with Dave in the winter of 1976. He lived in a shack and adjacent trailer without electricity or running water, in a sheltered spot beneath cottonwoods on a stream called Pike Creek. From his door you looked across sixty or seventy square miles of bleached playa desert south into the Trout Creek Mountains. It was dry country, with an annual temperature range of from one hundred degrees above to thirty-five degrees below zero. Dave subsisted mostly on canned foods, was kind toward his infrequent visitors, congenial, and he shared whatever he had without making a fool of himself.

I've met several men like Wallace in the West, but few of such varied background who were as clearheaded and energetic. When I asked him he agreed to a series of long interviews.

WHAT DAVE WALLACE, Bill Daniels and Odey Cassell represented I thought was vanishing. Before it was gone I wanted to speak with them, formally, as a writer; to make extensive notes; to try to elicit those things in them that were so attractive and give them names. For men who had had difficult times, without money and companionship, they were uncommonly free of bitterness. There was a desire in them to act to help when something went wrong rather than to assign blame, even when the trouble was over. When something went very wrong they reached down into a reservoir of implacable conviction, as a man puts his hands into a cold, clear basin of water. And they wrenched humor—impish in Odey, raw in Bill, laconic in Dave—out of the bleakest of these things.

I wanted to speak with them. Because there are lives, near and distant, wearing out too quickly, without plan or laughter.

I received word through a mutual friend the week I was making ready for the trip that Dave had died. He had apparently had a heart attack while driving down the dirt road past his place and had slumped across the steering wheel. The pickup had slowed, drifted off the road and come to rest against a thick tuft of rabbit brush. The engine must have run until it emptied the gas tank.

I made the three-hundred-mile drive a week later. His cabin had already been vandalized, by the same sort of people he had made welcome and fed from his meager garden.

A month later I learned of Bill Daniels's death in Dubois, Wyoming, at his brother's ranch. He had taken with him his extensive knowledge of the Sheepeaters. He had told me once that after seeing what had been done to other Indian sites he would die without telling the rest of what he knew.

When I read, a few weeks after this, Nettie's letter—". . . he hadn't been able to be out on the place for a long time, which he wanted to do so much . . . ."—I felt the loss of what Odey had been, and that his life, like Daniels's and Wallace's, was now irretrievable. The heart of my pain, and anger, I think, was that, unproclaimed, these men would have seemed to so many like failures.

I was, of course, very fond of them, as young men are fond of their grandfathers by blood or not; I realized just before they died that there was something of transcendent value in them, fragile and as difficult to extract as the color of a peach. I wanted to be able to have it and pass it on, and so their deaths left me burdened and confused, as though something had been stolen that I owned. The silence and obscurity that were so essential to their lives escaped me entirely. I could not leave them alone in their deaths.

IN THE DAYS FOLLOWING, no longer charged with a responsibility to describe them, I began to drift back to older, more personal feelings. One evening when I was out walking along the edge of a river that runs near my home I stopped and became absorbed in the swirling current of jade-colored water. Close by in the Douglas fir and cedar trees was a roaring, a white-water creek sheathed in mist where it hit the river in an explosion, and was absorbed in that massive, opaque flow. I took Nettie's letter out of my pocket, gently unfolded it and let it go.

The river flows I do not know how many miles, Odey, to another, which flows farther on to the Columbia, and on to the Pacific. There are whales there—they lead obscure and exemplary lives. They are as long as your barn, and speak with voices like the sound of the wind in the cave beneath your pasture. They are for the most part undisturbed. They seem to me to be at home.

# The Passing Wisdom of Birds

On the eighth of November, 1519, Hernando Cortés and four hundred Spanish soldiers marched self-consciously out of the city of Iztapalapa, Mexico, and started across the great Iztapalapan Causeway separating the lakes of Xochimilco and Chalco. They had been received the afternoon before in Iztapalapa as demigods; but they stared now in disbelief at what lay before them. Reflecting brilliantly on the vast plain of dark water like a landscape of sunlit chalk, its lines sharp as cut stone in the dustless air at 7200 feet, was the Aztec Byzantium—Tenochtitlán. Mexico City.

It is impossible to know what was in the facile, highly charged mind of Cortés that morning, anticipating his first meeting with the reluctant Montezuma; but Bernal Díaz, who was present, tells us what was on the minds of the soldiers. They asked each other was it *real*—gleaming Iztapalapa behind them, the smooth causeway beneath their feet, imposing Tenochtitlán ahead? The Spanish had been in the New World for twenty-seven years, but what they discovered in the Valley of Mexico that fall "had never been heard of or seen before, nor even dreamed about" in their world. What astounded them was not, solely, the extent and sophistication of the engineering that divided and encompassed the lakes surrounding Tenochtitlán; nor the evidence that a separate culture, utterly different from their own, pursued a complex life in this huge city. It was the depth and pervasiveness of the natural beauty before their senses.

The day before, they had strolled the spotless streets of Iztapalapa through plots of full-blossomed flowers, arranged in patterns and in colors pleasing to the eye; through irrigated fruit orchards; and into still groves of aromatic trees, like cedar. They sat in the shade of bright cotton awnings in quiet stone patios and marveled at the robustness and the well-tended orderliness of the vegetable gardens around them. Roses glowed against the lime-washed walls of the houses like garnets and alexandrites. In the hour before sunset, the cool, fragrant air was filled with the whirr and flutter of birds, and lit with birdsong.

That had been Iztapalapa. Mexico City, they thought, even as their leader dismounted that morning with solemn deliberation from that magical creature, the horse, to meet an advancing Montezuma ornately caparisoned in gold and silver and bird feathers—Mexico City, they thought as they approached, could only outdo Iztapalapa. And it did. With Montezuma's tentative welcome they were free to wander in its various precincts. Mexico City confirmed the image of a people gardening with meticulous care and with exquisite attention to line and detail at the edge of nature.

It is clear from Díaz's historical account that the soldiers were stunned by the physical beauty of Tenochtitlán. Venice came to their minds in comparison, because of its canals; but Venice was not as intensely fresh, as well lit as Mexico City. And there was not to be found in Venice, or in Salamanca or Paris for that matter, anything like the great aviaries where thousands of birds—white egrets, energetic wrens and thrushes, fierce accipiters, brilliantly colored parrots—were housed and tended. They were as captivating, as fabulous, as the displays of flowers: vermilion flycatchers, copper-tailed trogons, green jays, blue-throated hummingbirds, and summer tanagers. Great blue herons, brooding condors.

And throughout the city wild birds nested.

Even Cortés, intensely preoccupied with politics, with guiding a diplomacy of conquest in the region, noticed the birds. He was struck, too, by the affinity of the Mexican people for their gardens and for the measured and intricate flow of water through their city. He took time to write Charles V in Spain, describing it all.

Cortés's men, says Díaz, never seemed to tire of the arboretums, gardens, and aviaries in the months following their entry into the city. By June 1520, however, Cortés's psychological manipulation of Montezuma and a concomitant arrogance, greed, and disrespect on the part of the Spanish military force had become too much for the Mexicans, and they drove them out. Cortés, relentless and vengeful, returned to the Valley of Mexico eleven months later with a larger army and laid siege to the city. Canal by canal, garden by garden, home by home, he destroyed what he had described to Charles V as "the most beautiful city in the world." On June 16, in a move calculated to humiliate and frighten the Mexican people, Cortés set fire to the aviaries.

THE GROTESQUENESS and unmitigated violence of Cortés's act has come back to me repeatedly in reading of early European encounters with the landscapes of the New World, like a kind of darkness. The siege of Mexico City was fought barbarously on both sides; and the breathtaking parks and beautiful gardens of Mexico City, of course, stood hard by temples in which human life was regularly offered up to Aztec gods, by priests whose hair was matted with human gore and blood. No human culture has ever existed apart from its dark side. But what Cortés did, even under conditions of war, flies wildly in the face of a desire to find a dignified and honorable relationship with nature. It is an ambitious and vague longing, but one that has been with us for centuries, I think, and which today is a voice heard clearly from many different quarters—political science, anthropology, biology, philosophy. The desire is that, our colonial conquests of the human and natural world finally at an end, we will find our way back to a more equitable set of relationships with all we have subjugated. I say back because the early cultures from which Western civilization evolved, such as the Magdalenian phase of Cro-Magnon culture in Europe, apparently had a less contentious arrangement with nature before the development of agriculture in northern Mesopotamia, and the rise of cities.

The image of Cortés burning the aviaries is not simply for me an image of a kind of destructive madness that lies at the heart of imperialistic conquest; it is also a symbol of a long-term failure of Western civilization to recognize the intrinsic worth of the American landscape, and its potential value to human societies that have since come to be at odds with the natural world. While English, French, and Spanish explorers were cruising the eastern shores of America, dreaming of feudal fiefdoms, gold, and political advantage, the continent itself was, already, occupied in a complex way by more than five hundred different cultures, each of which regarded itself as living in some kind of enlightened intimacy with the land. A chance to rediscover the original wisdom inherent in the myriad sorts of human relationships possible with the nonhuman world, of course, was not of concern to us in the sixteenth century, as it is now, particularly to geographers, philosophers, historians, and ecologists. It would not in fact become clear for centuries that the metaphysics we had thrown out thousands of years before was still intact in tribal America. America offered us the opportunity to deliberate with historical perspective, to see if we wished to reclaim that metaphysics.

The need to reexamine our experience in the New World is, increasingly, a practical need. Contemporary American culture, founded on the original material wealth of the continent, on its timber, ores, and furs, has become a culture that devours the earth. Minerals, fresh water, darkness, tribal peoples, everything the land produces we now consume in prodigious amounts. There are at least two schools of thought on how to rectify this high rate of consumption, which most Western thinkers agree is unsustainable and likely wrongheaded if not disastrous. First, there are technical approaches. No matter how sophisticated or innovative these may be, however, they finally seem only clever or artful adjustments, not solutions. Secondly, we can consider a change in attitude toward nature, adopting a fundamentally different way of thinking about it than we have previously had, perhaps ever had as human beings. The insights of aboriginal peoples are of inestimable value here in rethinking our relationships with the natural world (i.e., in figuring out how to get ourselves back *into* it); but the solution to our plight, I think, is likely to be something no other culture has ever thought of, something over which !Kung, Inuit, Navajo, Walbiri, and the other traditions we have turned to for wisdom in the twentieth century will marvel at as well.

The question before us is how do we find a viable natural philosophy, one that places us again within the elements of our natural history. The answer, I believe, lies with wild animals.

## II

OVER THE PAST TEN YEARS it has been my privilege to spend time in the field in North America with biologists studying several different kinds of animals, including wolves, polar bears, mountain lions, seals, and whales. Of all that could be said about this exercise, about people watching animals, I would like to restrict myself to but one or two things. First, although such studies are scientific they are conducted by human beings whose individual speculations may take them out beyond the bounds of scientific inquiry. The animals they scrutinize may draw them back into an older, more intimate and less rational association with the local landscape. In this frame of mind, they may privately begin to question the methodology of Western science, especially its purported objectivity and its troublesome lack of heart. It may seem to them incapable of addressing questions they intuit are crucial. Even as they perceive its flaws, however, scientists continue to offer such studies as a dependable source of reliable information—and they are.

Science's flaws as a tool of inquiry are relatively minor, and it is further saved by its strengths.

Science's strength lies with its rigor and objectivity, and it is undoubtedly as rigorous as any system available to us. Even with its flaws (its failure, for example, to address disorderly or idiosyncratic behavior) field biology is as strong and reliable in its way as the collective wisdom of a hunting people actively involved with the land. The highest order of field work being done in biology today, then, from an elucidation of the way polar bears hunt ringed seals to working out the ecology of night-flying moths pollinating agaves in the Mojave Desert, forms part of the foundation for a modern realignment with the natural world. (The other parts of the foundation would include work done by anthropologists among hunter-gatherer people and studies by natural geographers; philosophical work in the tradition of Aldo Leopold and Rachel Carson; and the nearly indispensable element of personal experience.)

I often search out scientific reports to read; many are based on years of research and have been patiently thought through. Despite my regard, however, I read with caution, for I cannot rid myself of the thought that, even though it is the best theoretical approach we have, the process is not perfect. I have participated in some of this type of work and know that innocent mistakes are occasionally made in the data. I understand how influential a misleading coincidence can become in the overall collection of data; how unconsciously the human mind can follow a teasing parallel. I am cautious, too, for even more fundamental reasons. It is hard to say exactly what any animal is *doing*. It is impossible to know when or where an event in an animal's life begins or ends. And our human senses confine us to realms that may contain only a small part of the information produced in an event. Something critical could be missing and we would not know. And as far as the experiments themselves are concerned, although we can design and carry out thousands of them, no animal can ever be described as the sum of these experiments. And, finally, though it is possible to write precisely about something, this does not automatically mean one is accurate.

The scientific approach is flawed, therefore, by its imposition of a subjective framework around animal behavior; but it only fails, really, because it is incomplete. We would be rash, using this approach exclusively, to claim to understand any one animal, let alone the environment in which that animal is evolving. Two remedies to this dilemma of the partially perceived animal suggest themselves. One, obviously, is to turn to the long-term field observations of non-Western cultural traditions. These non-Aristotelian, non-Cartesian, non-Baconian views of wild animals are stimulating, challenging, and, like a good bibliography, heuristic, pointing one toward discovery. (They are also problematic in that, for example, they do not take sufficiently into account the full range of behavior of migratory animals and they have a highly nonlinear [though ultimately, possibly, more correct] understanding of population biology.)

A second, much less practiced remedy is to cultivate within ourselves a sense of mystery—to see that the possibilities for an expression of life in any environment, or in any single animal, are larger than we can predict or understand, and that this is all right. Biology should borrow here from quantum physics, which accepts the premise that, under certain circumstances, the observer can be deceived. Quantum physics, with its ambiguous particles and ten-dimensional universes, is a branch of science that has in fact returned us to a state of awe with nature, without threatening our intellectual capacity to analyze complex events.

IF IT IS TRUE that modern people desire a new relationship with the natural world, one that is not condescending, manipulative, and purely utilitarian; and if the foundation upon which the relationship is to be built is as I suggest—a natural history growing largely out of science and the insights of native peoples—then a staggering task lies before us.

The initial steps to be taken seem obvious. First, we must identify and protect those regions where landscapes largely undisturbed by human technology remain intact. Within these ecosystems lie blueprints for the different patterns of life that have matured outside the pervasive influence of myriad Western technologies (though no place on earth has escaped their influence entirely). We can contemplate and study endlessly the natural associations here, and draw from these smaller universes a sophisticated wisdom about process and event, and about evolution. Second, we need to subscribe a great public support to the discipline of field biology. Third, we need to seek an introduction to the reservoirs of intelligence that native cultures have preserved in both oral tradition and in their personal experience with the land, the highly complex detail of a way of life not yet torn entirely from the fabric of nature.

We must, too, look out after the repositories of our own long-term cultural wisdom more keenly. Our libraries, which preserve the best of what we have to say about ourselves and nature, are under siege in an age of cost-benefit analysis. We need to immerse ourselves thoughtfully, too, in what is being written and produced on tape and film, so that we become able to distinguish again between truthful expression and mere entertainment. We need to do this not only for our own sake but so that our children, who too often have only the half-eclipsed lives of zoo animals or the contrived dramas of television wildlife adventure before them, will know that this heritage is disappearing and what we are apt to lose with it.

What disappears with a debasement of wild landscapes is more than genetic diversity, more than a homeland for Henry Beston's "other nations," more, to be perfectly selfish, than a source of future medical cures for human illness or a chance for personal revitalization on a wilderness trip. We stand to lose the focus of our ideals. We stand to lose our sense of dignity, of compassion, even our sense of what we call God. The philosophy of nature we set aside eight thousand years ago in the Fertile Crescent we can, I think, locate again and greatly refine in North America. The New World is a landscape still overwhelming in the vigor of its animals and plants, resonant with mystery. It encourages, still, an enlightened response toward indigenous cultures that differ from our own, whether Aztecan, Lakotan, lupine, avian, or invertebrate. By broadening our sense of the intrinsic worth of life and by cultivating respect for other ways of moving toward perfection, we may find a sense of resolution we have been looking for, I think, for centuries.

TWO PRACTICAL STEPS occur to me. Each by itself is so small I hesitate to set it forth; but to say nothing would be cowardly, and both appear to me to be reasonable, a beginning. They also acknowledge an obvious impediment: to bridge the chasm between a colonial attitude toward the land and a more filial relationship with it takes time. The task has always been, and must be, carried into the next generation.

The first thought I would offer is that each university and college in the country establish the position of university naturalist, a position to be held by a student in his or her senior year and passed on at the end of the year to another student. The university naturalist would be responsible for establishing and maintaining a natural history of the campus, would confer with architects and grounds keepers, escort guests, and otherwise look out after the nonhuman elements of the campus, their relationships to human beings, and the preservation of this knowledge. Though the position itself might be honorary and unsalaried, the student would receive substantial academic credit for his or her work and would be provided with a budget to conduct research, maintain a library, and produce an occasional paper. Depending on his or her gifts and personality, the university naturalist might elect to teach a course or to speak at some point during the academic year. In concert with the university archivist and university historian, the university naturalist would seek to protect the relationships-in-time that define a culture's growth and ideals.

A second suggestion is more difficult to implement, but no less important than a system of university naturalists. In recent years several American and British publishers have developed plans to reprint in an extended series classic works of natural history. These plans should be pursued; the list of books should include not only works of contemporary natural history but early works by such people as Thomas Nuttal and William Bartram, so that the project has historical depth. It should also include books by nonscientists who have immersed themselves "beyond reason" in the world occupied by animals and who have emerged with stunning reports, such as J. A. Baker's *The Peregrine.* And books that offer us a resounding and affecting vision of the landscape, such as John Van Dyke's *The Desert.* It should also include the writing of anthropologists who have worked, or are working, with the native peoples of North America to define an indigenous natural history, such as Richard Nelson's *Make Prayers to the Raven.* And a special effort should be made to unearth those voices that once spoke eloquently for parts of the country the natural history of which is now too often overlooked, or overshadowed, by a focus on western or northern North American ecosystems: the pine barrens of New Jersey, the Connecticut River Valley, the White Mountains of New Hampshire, the remnant hardwood forests of Indiana and Ohio, the Outer Banks, the relictual prairies of Texas, and the mangrove swamps and piney woods of Georgia.

Such a collection, it seems to me, should be assembled with several thoughts in mind. It should be inexpensive so that the books can fall easily into the hands of young people. It should document the extraordinary variety of natural ecosystems in North America, and reflect the great range of dignified and legitimate human response to them. And it should make clear that human beings belong in these landscapes, that they, too, are a part of the earth's natural history.

III

THE IMAGE I carry of Cortés setting fire to the aviaries in Mexico City that June day in 1521 is an image I cannot rid myself of. It stands, in my mind, for a fundamental lapse of wisdom in the European conquest of America, an underlying trouble in which political conquest, personal greed, revenge, and national pride outweigh what is innocent, beautiful, serene, and defenseless—the birds. The incineration of these creatures 450 years ago is not something that can be rectified today. Indeed, one could argue, the same oblivious irreverence is still with us, among those who would ravage and poison the earth to sustain the economic growth of Western societies. But Cortés's act can be transcended. It is possible to fix in the mind that heedless violence, the hysterical cries of the birds, the stench of death, to look it square in the face and say that there is more to us than this, this will not forever distinguish us among the other cultures. It is possible to imagine that on the far side of the Renaissance and the Enlightenment we can recover the threads of an earlier wisdom.

Again I think of the animals, because of the myriad ways in which they have helped us since we first regarded each other differently. They offered us early models of rectitude and determination in adversity, which we put into stories. The grace of a moving animal, in some ineluctable way, kindles still in us a sense of imitation. They continue to produce for us a sense of the Other: to encounter a truly wild animal on its own ground is to know the defeat of thought, to feel reason overpowered. The animals have fed us; and the cultures of the great hunters particularly—the bears, the dogs, and the cats—have provided the central metaphors by which we have taken satisfaction in our ways and explained ourselves to strangers.

Cortés's soldiers, on their walks through the gleaming gardens of Tenochtitlán, would have been as struck by the flight paths of songbirds as we are today. In neither a horizontal nor a vertical dimension do these pathways match the line and scale of human creation, within which the birds dwell. The corridors they travel are curved around some other universe. When the birds passed over them, moving across the grain of sunlight, the soldiers must have stopped occasionally to watch, as we do. It is the birds' independence from predictable patterns of human design that draws us to them. In the birds' separate but related universe we are able to sense hope for ourselves. Against a background of the familiar, we recognize with astonishment a new pattern.

In such a moment, pausing to take in the flight of a flock of birds passing through sunshine and banking gracefully into a grove of trees, it is possible to move beyond a moment in the Valley of Mexico when we behaved as though we were insane.

## About the Author

Barry Lopez was born in Port Chester, New York, in 1945. He grew up in southern California and in New York City and has lived for the past twenty years in rural Oregon. He is the author of *Arctic Dreams, Of Wolves and Men,* and several collections of fiction, including *Winter Count* and *River Notes.* A contributing editor to *Harper's* and *North American Review,* he has received an Award in Literature from the American Academy and Institute of Arts and Letters, the American Book Award, and the John Burroughs Medal, among other honors.